Early Learning

Managing an Effective Early Childhood Classroom

Author
Wendy Koza

Contributing Author
Jodene Smith, M.A.

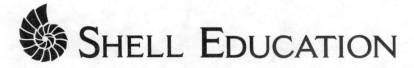
SHELL EDUCATION

Editor
Mary Rosenberg

Project Manager
Jodene Smith, M.A.

Assistant Editor
Leslie Huber, M.A.

Editorial Director
Dona Herweck Rice

Editor-in-Chief
Sharon Coan, M.S.Ed.

Editorial Manager
Gisela Lee, M.A.

Creative Director
Lee Aucoin

Cover Design
Amy Couch

Artists
Anna Clark
Timothy J. Bradley

Illustration Manager
Timothy J. Bradley

Imaging
Phil Garcia
Don Tran

Publisher
Corinne Burton, M.A.Ed

Standards Compendium, Copyright 2004 McREL

Shell Educational Publishing
5301 Oceanus Drive
Huntington Beach, California 92649
http://www.shelleducation.com
ISBN 978-1-4258-0052-9
© 2007 Shell Educational Publishing

Table of Contents

Introduction and Research

Welcome to the world of the preschool child. Preschool children love to play, get dirty, and discover. The ideas and suggestions in this book will help you create an inviting environment and a quality program that will meet all the needs of the children in your class.

This book is divided into six sections. The first section, *The Preschool Child*, covers the development of young children. Preschool teachers need to be cognizant of individual children's developmental levels, chronological ages, and general developmental stages. In addition, knowledge of infant-toddler theories and developmentally appropriate practice for toddlers (Gilbert, 2001) is needed. Included in this section is a comparison of two preschool-aged children, a description of the varying preschool philosophies, and checklists to use when assessing the children's development.

The National Association for the Education of Young Children advocates educational practices that allow for an interactive approach to learning and teacher-positive guidance techniques (NAYEC, 1996). An understanding of the role of development in early childhood education is paramount to the child's success. The assessments and information in this section follow the principles of leading pioneers in the field of early childhood development to include Italian physician Maria Montessori and Swiss psychologist Jean Piaget. Montessori emphasized the teaching of practical life skills and sensory-based manipulative materials at increasing levels of complexity (Gartell, 2007). Her philosophy is highly regarded today in creating a developmentally-appropriate preschool program. Piaget's clinical, rather than classroom centered, approach to understanding development is recognized as a critical component for educators working with young children. He describes the patterns children follow in learning about the world, and he confirmed that children follow stages of development in their learning (Piaget, 1973). The need for educators working with preschool-aged children to understand the importance of early childhood development, and developmentally appropriate practice in the classroom is critical to the success of any preschool program.

The Classroom and Materials is the second section. It includes information on room arrangement and organization, as well as activity centers. Discovery centers in preschool foster observational and problem-solving skills through the exploration and examination of objects (Chrisman, 2005). Teaching preschool using a center-based approach is considered best practice. When setting up a preschool classroom, the expectations in the environment should be clear (Friedman, 2005). The floor plans included in this section clearly demonstrate the most effective room arrangement to foster learning among preschool children. Developing effective activity centers in the early childhood classroom results in measurable, meaningful educational outcomes, and is the physical embodiment of developmentally appropriate practice (Gartrell, 2007). This section includes examples of floor plans, suggestions for how to maintain and order supplies for your class, and checklists of materials that should be in each center.

Introduction and Research (cont.)

The third section, *The Preschool Day*, covers how a day in a preschool program looks. More than 100 years ago Montessori recognized that young children need a sense of order and continuity (Gartrell, 2007). Children feel secure and benefit from a structured and routine environment. Developing a daily schedule that includes consistency, smooth transitions, and routine is a critical element in a preschool program. Descriptions of the various components of a preschool schedule are included in this section, as well as suggestions for establishing routines and a schedule.

The fourth section is *Planning*. Find out how to create long-term, short-term, and daily lesson plans, along with examples and tools that will assist you in creating a successful year. It is helpful to plan lessons in a center-based classroom using themes. Integrating subject matter in themes enables the child to find meaning in learning (Gartrell, 2007). The tools in this section will allow you to develop lesson plans that foster development and learning through meaningful activities. Field trips can serve a variety of purposes, such as exposing children to new things or helping children to see familiar things in new ways (DeMarie, 2001). Ideas and suggestions on planning field trips are also provided in this section.

Classroom Management, the fifth section of the book, covers parent communication, volunteers, record keeping, and behavior. Parent involvement greatly affects student achievement (Turner, 2000). In this section you will learn the most effective ways to keep parents informed and engage them as useful volunteers in the classroom. Examples of classroom newsletters and monthly calendars are included. Effective classroom management also involves managing behavior in a positive way. This section provides methods to encourage conflict resolution, develop classroom rules, and allow children to become responsible for their actions and behaviors. Teachers who are leaders recognize the importance of sincere acknowledgement of a child's efforts and progress (Gartrell, 2007). The tools in this section provide guidance for you to effectively manage your preschool classroom.

The sixth and final section is *Addressing Skills*, where you will find ways to focus on the individual child and his or her growth, different types of assessments, and suggestions for scheduling successful parent-teacher conferences. Also included are ways to set foundations for reading. Teachers today are held accountable for student achievement. Assessment of learning is critical for future lesson planning based on the individual needs of the child. This section describes portfolios, anecdotal records, and observations as forms of assessment. The increasing emphasis on accountability in early care and education has created an opportunity for programs to revisit their child assessment practices. (Grisham-Brown, Hallam, and Brookshire, 2006). Using this book you will be able to create authentic assessments to maximize student learning. You will also learn strategies to help you prepare for parent-teacher conferences to develop a positive parent-teacher relationship.

Introduction and Research (cont.)

Throughout the book are "Teacher Tips" that provide quick and easy ideas and suggestions for improving a preschool program. The ideas, set apart in a chalkboard at the side or bottom of the page, are tried-and-true tips from an experienced preschool teacher, that you will want to be sure to include in your preschool program.

As a preschool teacher, you have the task of introducing young children to the world of school. You will need to plan meaningful activities for the children in your classroom. Children will feel successful when they are exposed to meaningful experiences that allow them to discover in a safe, non-judgmental environment, along with receiving accurate feedback (Fromberg, 1998). The activities and ideas in this book support the importance of play and meaningful experiences. This book will provide the teacher of young children with the foundations for creating an excellent preschool program. By implementing the ideas in this book, you will be creating a quality program that will lead to many years of success for all the children in your class.

Physical Development

Parents send their children to preschool for many different reasons. Some parents enroll their young children in preschool for the cognitive stimulation, and others for the social interaction among children of the same age. No matter what the reason, your job is to consider and educate the whole child. A child makes the most dramatic growth in all areas of development from birth to five years of age. Consider a newborn child: he or she will learn to roll, crawl, walk, talk, and use the bathroom, and eventually learn to play organized sports and write short stories, all within a few short years.

The physical, cognitive, linguistic, social, and emotional development in each child will proceed at an individual rate. Not all children learn to walk at one year old. Some learn as early as nine months, and others as late as 14 months. When discussing at which developmental stage children should be performing, both the age range and the individual child should be considered. All children will follow the same sequence in the development of each skill. Some steps will take a long time to master, while others will be mastered in just a few short days. For example, a child will walk before running or will scribble in a circular pattern before making a circle.

Stages of Development

A One-Year-Old Child	A Two-Year-Old Child
• He or she is considered a young toddler or an older infant. • His or her life is full of risks and new experiences. • He or she will begin eating regular table food and begin walking.	• He or she is considered a toddler. • Toddlers are often considered a handful. • He or she will be testing boundaries and limits. • He or she will be learning to communicate verbally.
A Three-Year-Old Child	**A Four-Year-Old Child**
• He or she is considered a preschool child. • He or she will learn to use the toilet independently. • He or she can now speak in sentences and communicate with peers. • He or she will now begin to develop an attention span of about 10 minutes. • He or she should know most colors and shapes and begin recognizing his or her name.	• He or she is considered a prekindergartner. • He or she should now have an attention span of 10 to 15 minutes. • He or she may even be able to write his or her name.

Just before entering kindergarten around the age of five, he or she should:

- Know and be able to write most of the letters of the alphabet.
- Have one-to-one correspondence.
- Have some understanding of abstract concepts.

Physical Development (cont.)

The physical development of a prekindergarten child doesn't differ that much between girls and boys. From the ages of two to six, girls are only slightly smaller and lighter than boys. The average height and weight for a five-year-old girl is 43 inches and 40 pounds, and the average height and weight for a five-year-old boy is 44 inches and 45 pounds. When a child turns three, the muscle tone increases and body fat decreases, making the child appear slimmer. Remember that growth patterns are individual and will vary from child to child.

Gross Motor

Gross motor refers to a child's ability to move the entire body and his or her spatial awareness.

- Gross-motor or large-motor skills are: hopping, jumping, skipping, running, and climbing.
- By the age of four, his or her play and gross-motor activities will become more adventurous and he or she will take more risks.
- Gross-motor development takes practice. Encourage daily exercise of the large-motor skills through the use of outside equipment, such as: balance beams, balls, bikes, and fast-paced activities. This will improve coordination.
- Encourage him or her to practice locomotor skills inside by moving his or her body to various types of music.

Fine Motor

Fine motor refers to a child's ability to use and have control over the small muscles in his or her hands.

- Fine-motor skills are essential in being able to color, write, paint, and cut.
- His or her fine-motor development changes drastically from the age of three to the age of five.
- At three years of age, he or she will be able to string large beads and stack three blocks but will still struggle and will try to fit small manipulatives into incorrect openings.
- At five years of age, he or she will be able to put small puzzle pieces together, trace around an object, draw shapes, and hold writing implements appropriately, and may be able to write letters.

Physical Development (cont.)

Physical (Gross-Motor Skills) Development Checklist for a Four- to Five-Year-Old

Child's Name _____

- ❑ Understands *over, under, through*
- ❑ Can work within own space
- ❑ Balance beam
  - ❑ walks forward on beam
  - ❑ walks backward on beam
  - ❑ walks over objects on beam
- ❑ Jumping skills
  - ❑ jumps on trampoline
  - ❑ jumps rope
  - ❑ completes standing broad jump
- ❑ Pumps on swing
- ❑ Locomotor skills
  - ❑ runs
  - ❑ gallops
  - ❑ hops on one foot
- ❑ Crab-walks

- ❑ Handling a ball
  - ❑ throws a ball underhand
  - ❑ throws a ball overhand
  - ❑ bounces a ball
  - ❑ catches a ball from four feet away
  - ❑ throws beanbags at a target
- ❑ Kicking a ball
  - ❑ kicks a stationary ball
  - ❑ kicks a rolling ball
- ❑ Rides a tricycle
- ❑ Hangs from a bar
- ❑ Performs forward somersaults
- ❑ Walks down stairs, alternating feet
- ❑ Can cross the midline when batting
- ❑ Skips

Physical Development (cont.)

Physical (Fine-Motor Skills) Development Checklist for a Four- to Five-Year-Old

Child's Name _____

- ❏ Has established handedness
- ❏ Attempts to copy letters
- ❏ Shows control of small muscles in coloring, painting, cutting, and writing
- ❏ Using scissors
  - ❏ can use scissors appropriately
  - ❏ can cut along a straight line
  - ❏ can cut following a zigzag line
- ❏ Dressing skills
  - ❏ can zip
  - ❏ can button
  - ❏ can snap
  - ❏ can buckle
  - ❏ will attempt to tie shoes
- ❏ Using manipulatives
  - ❏ can use small manipulatives successfully
  - ❏ can stack small blocks
  - ❏ completes 10-piece puzzle
  - ❏ can string beads
  - ❏ can place small pegs into holes
- ❏ Draws a person with clear and distinct body parts (head, body, legs, arms)

Cognitive Development

Cognitive Ability

Cognitive ability refers to a child's ability to concentrate on an activity, complete a task, and recognize shapes, colors, classification, and eventually letters of the alphabet. Remember that children learn in different ways. The key to helping a child develop cognitive skills is exposure. Provide the children with hands-on activities and opportunities to discover and rediscover. When children discover something on their own, it creates meaning and stays in their long-term memories. For example, two children are working at the sensory table that has been filled with water. One child fills a short, fat container with water and then pours it into a tall, skinny container. The other child is watching, and together they discover that the two containers are different sizes and shapes but hold the same amount of water. This kind of discovery also helps develop language and provides social learning opportunities. Giving children situations in which they are to sort, count, and manipulate objects significantly helps cognitive development.

Cognitive Abilities of a Prekindergartner

Prekindergarten children should be able to complete certain simple tasks.

- A four- or five-year-old child who begins to assemble a puzzle or work on a matching or sorting activity should be able to tend to the task until it is complete.
- A five-year-old should be able to recite the alphabet, recognize most of the letters, and possibly recognize simple words in print. These are the beginning stages of learning how to read.

As children grow, so do their abstract thinking skills.

- A two- or three-year-old will have difficulty understanding the concept of time. The word *tomorrow* refers to events in the future, and *yesterday* refers to events in the past.
- By the time children reach age five, they have a simple understanding of time. They will understand the parts of a day (morning, noon, and night) and will be able to distinguish the seasons.

The more exposure you provide, including opportunities for hands-on experiences, the more children will naturally increase their abilities to think abstractly, show concentration, and make cognitive growth.

Cognitive Development (cont.)

Cognitive Development Checklist for a
Four- to Five-Year-Old

Child's Name _____

❏ Shows rote counting ability	❏ Recognizes numerals not in sequence
❏ Writes numerals	❏ Understands positional terms (first–fifth)
Names geometric shapes ❏ circle ❏ square ❏ rectangle ❏ oval ❏ heart ❏ star ❏ diamond ❏ octagon	Recognizes basic colors ❏ red ❏ orange ❏ yellow ❏ green ❏ blue ❏ purple ❏ pink ❏ brown ❏ black ❏ white
❏ Makes comparisons as to size and quantity	❏ Recognizes and writes own name
❏ Recognizes friends' names	❏ Recognizes capital letters
❏ Recognizes lowercase letters	❏ Writes letters of the alphabet
❏ Recognizes letter sounds	❏ Recognizes some sight words
❏ Contributes to group stories	❏ Expresses ideas in complete sentences

Language Development

Language Development

Language development refers to a child's ability to speak, read, and write. A child's ability to speak depends as much on individual development as learning to walk. A two-year-old child will be able to say one or two words. Eventually, he or she will begin putting words together to create phrases and sentences. By the time the child is five years old, his or her vocabulary will increase to several thousand words. He or she will be able to hold lengthy conversations with adults as well as create simple stories. Learning to speak and develop language occurs over a few short years. Encouraging children to speak to one another and to you is important in developing this skill.

Promoting Language Development

There are several things you can do to help with language development.

- Give the child time to think about what he or she wants to say. Often, parents and adults are in a hurry and say what the child means instead of giving the child the time to say it for himself or herself.
- Stuttering also may begin to develop somewhere around three or four. Children at this age often think faster than they can speak, which results in a stutter. If you or the parents feel that the stuttering is becoming an issue, contact the child's doctor and have an evaluation done. Most of the time, children outgrow stuttering as they get older. Slow down and give the child the gift of time.
- Actively listen to what the child is saying. If the child says, "I heard a helicopter today," then ask the child, "Where do you think the helicopter was going?" Give the child time to respond.
- Encourage the child to talk about things he or she knows about. Share Day and show-and-tell are perfect opportunities for the child to show and talk about something he or she has brought from home. It is easy for a child to talk about something with which he or she is familiar.

teacher tip

Labeling items in your classroom also promotes language. Use pictures and/or words to identify where things belong in the classroom or what goes inside each bin, container, or cubby. Use the proper names of objects—for example, watercolor paints, tempera paints.

Language Development (cont.)

Reading Aloud

Reading to your class on a daily basis is important because it models the importance of literature and introduces the children to new words. Exposing your class to different types of literature such as chapter books, poems, and rhyming books also helps children develop language. Reading is a fun and enjoyable activity to encourage learning.

Encourage your class to participate in reading instead of being passive listeners. Prompt the children to ask questions and predict what might happen next in the story. This kind of interactive reading helps foster a love of reading as children move into adulthood.

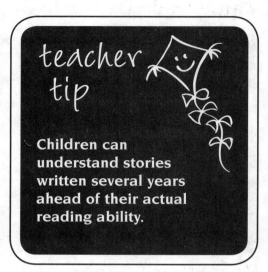

teacher tip

Children can understand stories written several years ahead of their actual reading ability.

Hearing and Language Development

When children are learning to speak, they repeat the sounds they are hearing. A child can't repeat words or sounds properly if he or she is not hearing them correctly. Language development and the ability to speak are dependent on a child being able to hear.

Public Law 98-199

- This law provides financial incentives to children who require extra services.
- It applies to any child from birth to age three with special needs.
- Special needs are: hearing loss, vision impairment, physical impairments, and mental disabilities.

Public Law 94-142

IDEA (Individual with Disabilities Education Act)

- This law assures all children a free and appropriate public education.
- It is for individuals ages 3 to 21.

If you have a child in your class whose speech is difficult to understand or sounds as if he or she is speaking through his or her nose, suggest to the parents that they have the child's hearing tested by a pediatrician. After an initial assessment of the child's hearing, the family may be referred to a specialist, and the school district will need to be notified.

Social-Emotional Development

The Family Dynamics

In today's society, there are a number of different family dynamics. These situations are major factors affecting a child's social-emotional growth. Some types of family situations are:

- Two-parent families with the mother and father
- Separated or divorced parents who share the responsibility of raising the child together
- Single parents
- Same-gender parents
- Blended families
- Grandparents who are raising the child
- Families where one parent is in the workforce while the other parent stays home with the child

As a teacher, you need to be open-minded and supportive of each of these families.

Parenting Styles

Each family may have different parenting styles and choose to raise the child in a different way.

- You will come across parents who have all the control over the child and do not let him or her make decisions or allow the child to be independent. These children will struggle with new experiences and social situations because the parent is not there to tell them what to say or do.
- Then there are parents who let the child do whatever he or she wants. This child will expect to get whatever he or she wants. These parents are often trying to be the child's friend, or do not want to see their "baby" grow up. They don't want the child to be mad at them or hear them say, "I don't like you." These children seldom have respect for teachers or for the other children in the class. They are still egocentric.
- Finally, you will come across parents who have established limits and expectations for the child but still allow him or her to be independent and make choices. These parents are firm and loving at the same time. These children understand rules and limits but are still able to make decisions on their own.

All these parenting and family situations affect the social-emotional development of the young child, and you will come across all of them as you teach.

The Child's Personality

The personality of a child will also affect how the child functions in the classroom. You will have children in your class who may be quiet and seldom speak. There will be other children who are social butterflies and talk to everyone all the time. Children naturally have different personalities just as adults do. As the classroom teacher, you can have a positive impact on each child's self-esteem and confidence. Get to know each child as an individual by spending some quality one-on-one time with him or her.

Social-Emotional Development (cont.)

Experiences

When a child enters your classroom, you know only what you have been told by the parents. The parents' interpretation of what happened in any given situation may not reflect the true feelings of the child. You may be told by the parents, "Johnny was at an in-home day care. He was the oldest child there and now I feel he is ready to be around children of his own age." What the parent just told you is true, but how does the child feel about the change and the old environment? Was he overlooked because he was the oldest? Was the in-home provider like a second mom with whom he had a strong bond, and now he feels a sense of loss? You do not know what type of experience the child had in any previous situation. All the child's previous experiences, negative and positive, affect his or her social-emotional development. You need to be just as comforting and supportive of the social butterfly as you would be of the child who needs more support.

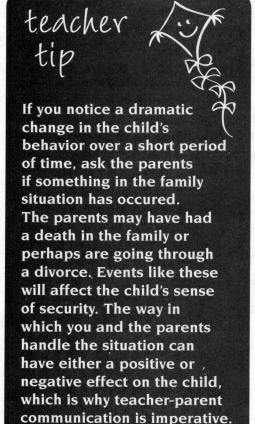

teacher tip

If you notice a dramatic change in the child's behavior over a short period of time, ask the parents if something in the family situation has occured. The parents may have had a death in the family or perhaps are going through a divorce. Events like these will affect the child's sense of security. The way in which you and the parents handle the situation can have either a positive or negative effect on the child, which is why teacher-parent communication is imperative.

Children at Play

As young children develop and change, so does their play.

- You will find a group of two- or three-year-olds playing in a sandbox. You might think they are playing together. They are actually involved in parallel play.
- Parallel play is playing with the same tools and mimicking each other. These children are not playing together, just simply using the same materials.
- As the children grow, their play will eventually change to play that requires conversation and interaction such as role-playing and organized games.

As an educator, your responsibility is to accept the children the way they are and to help each child develop a sense of self and positive self-esteem. Encourage the children to be good friends and make good choices. Help the class develop a sense of a classroom community, where every child counts and everyone has feelings and opinions that will be considered. This is a great place to start in helping the social-emotional development of the children.

Observations of Alyssa and Sami

Here are two observations on two unrelated children.

- These children are exactly one year apart in age, to the day.
- They attend the same preschool and are the same gender.
- Both children live with their respective mother and father.

Alyssa: Five years, three months

- She has attended group-care settings since she was six months old.
- She is the older of two children.
- She is going to enter kindergarten in three months.

Sami: Four years, three months

- She has been in a group-care setting for one year.
- She is the youngest of five children.
- She has another year of preschool before entering kindergarten.

	Alyssa	Sami
Fine Motor		
• Established handedness	Right-handed	Right-handed
• Controls small muscles (coloring, painting, cutting, writing)	Does well.	Yes, she holds the crayon correctly.
• Uses scissors appropriately	Yes	Yes
• Ability to zip, button, snap, and buckle	Does all with ease.	Not yet
• Attempts to tie shoes	Very close; just needs a bit more practice.	No, and didn't know how to start.
• Uses small manipulatives successfully	Chooses manipulatives often.	Yes, only uses large ones.
Speech Development		
• Has clear and distinct speech	Yes, and is comfortable talking with others.	Yes, she is easy to understand.
Social Growth and Work Habits		
• Talks freely with other children	Yes, she is comfortable talking with others.	Yes
• Works and plays cooperatively with others	She is learning to work problems out independently.	Yes, she is very social and has many friends.
• Participates in organized group activities	Yes, she is always eager to participate.	Only with small groups.
• Shows respect and consideration of others	Yes, and she is respectful of adults.	Yes
• Practices self-control	Yes	Yes
• Follows classroom rules	Knows all the rules and follows them easily.	Yes, with ease.
• Performs simple classroom chores	Enjoys helping and is self-motivated.	Yes

Observations of Alyssa and Sami (cont.)

	Alyssa	Sami
Social Growth and Work Habits (cont.)		
• Demonstrates self-confidence	Very much.	Yes
• Shows concentration in group activities	Usually; sometimes she needs redirecting.	Yes
• Contributes to group discussions	Yes, she always has a lot to offer.	Yes
• Follows oral directions	Yes, two- and three-step directions.	Two-step directions
• Works independently	Yes, with good focus.	Yes
• Takes time with projects	Yes; lots of detail, and stays with project until it is finished.	Yes
Mathematical Skills		
• Shows rote-counting ability	She can count to 39.	1–14
• Recognizes numerals not in sequence	1–11	Not yet
• Writes numerals	One through 11. The two and three are reversed.	Not yet
• Understands positional terms (first–fifth)	She understands the concepts of *first* through *fifth*.	Not yet
• Names geometric shapes: circle, square, rectangle, oval, heart, star, diamond, octagon	She knew all that were asked.	She knew circle, square, heart, star, and diamond.
• Makes comparisons as to size and quantity	She knows *small, medium, large, less, more*.	Knew *empty* and *full*.
Reading and Language Arts		
• Recognizes and writes own name	Yes, first and last names.	Recognizes Sami, but not Samantha.
• Recognizes friends' names	Yes, all the children in her class.	Some
• Recognizes basic colors: red, orange, yellow, green, blue, purple, pink, brown, black, white	Yes, knew all that were asked.	She knew red, orange, yellow, green, blue, purple, white, black, gray, and pink. She said gray when shown the color brown.
• Recognizes uppercase letters	Yes, all 26.	Not yet. She did use letter names but did not match the appropriate letter.
• Recognizes lowercase letters	Yes, all 26.	Not yet. She said, "I don't know."
• Writes letters of the alphabet	Yes, all 26 letters.	Not yet
• Recognizes rhyming words	Yes	No
• Recognizes letter sounds	Knows most of them.	Not yet
• Recognizes some sight words	She knows: *what, dog, cat, happy* (good start).	Just her name and names of a few friends.
• Contributes to group stories	Often	Yes, enjoys telling stories.
• Expresses ideas in complete sentences	Yes, her communication and language skills are great.	Yes, simple sentences.

Observations of Alyssa and Sami (cont.)

	Alyssa	Sami
Gross Motor Development		
Body-Spatial Awareness— understanding one's body and how it works in relation to itself, other objects, and other people.		
• Understands *over, under, through*	Yes, demonstrated all three.	Yes, demonstrated all three.
• Can work within own space	Easily	Yes, she is aware of personal body space.
Balance		
• Walks forward on balance beam	Yes, with ease.	Yes, with focus.
• Walks backward on balance beam	Yes, with ease.	Not yet
• Walks over objects on beam	Yes	Yes, she went slowly.
Dynamic Balance—maintaining control of the body when suspended in the air for a length of time.		
• Jumps on trampoline	Yes	Yes
• Skips	Yes	Not yet, but can gallop well.
• Jumps rope	Yes	Not yet
• Standing broad jump	Yes	Not yet
Laterality—using one side, opposite sides, or upper and lower parts of the body in a smooth, rhythmic manner.		
• Pumps on swing	Yes, she can even self-start.	Not yet
• Runs	Yes, with ease.	Yes, with ease.
• Gallops	Yes	Yes, with ease.
• Monkey-walks	Yes	Yes
• Hops on two feet	Nothing noted for Alyssa.	Yes
• Hops on one foot	Right and left	Right and left. When asked to hop on one foot, she was unsure. She wanted to hold on to the table. After she let go, she only hopped one time.
• Crab-walks	Yes	Yes
• Bear-walks on a ladder	Yes	She was unsure and seemed uncomfortable.

Observations of Alyssa and Sami (cont.)

	Alyssa	Sami
Gross Motor Development (cont.)		
Tracking—The ability to perform tasks involving objects and people outside one's own space		
• Keeps a balloon in the air	Yes, she hit it back up in the air five times.	Yes, three times.
• Catches a ball from four feet away	Yes	No, she was able to catch the ball from two feet away.
Center Line—The ability to perform tasks that require the crossing of the midline with another object		
• Cross-walk	Yes	Not yet
• Can cross the midline when batting	Yes	Not yet; she moved her entire upper body.
Eye-hand/eye-foot—The ability to use the eyes, hands, and feet together to accomplish a given task.		
• Throws a ball underhand	Yes	Yes, and was able to hit a target.
• Throws a ball overhand	Yes	Yes, and was able to hit a target.
• Throws beanbags at a target	Yes, with good aim and focus.	Yes, with ease.
• Rides a tricycle	Yes	Yes
• Kicks a stationary ball	Yes	Yes
• Kicks a rolling ball	Yes	Needs a bit more practice.
• Bounces a ball	Yes	One time only; needs more practice.
Upper Body Strength and Flexibility		
• Hangs from a bar	Yes	No, was not comfortable letting body hang.
• Seal-walks	Yes	Needs practice. She kept lifting up her lower body and using her legs.
• Performs forward somersaults	Yes	Yes

Observations of Alyssa and Sami (cont.)

Alyssa's Summary

Motor Development

Her fine- and gross-motor skills are well developed. She uses scissors appropriately, holds a pencil correctly, and can snap, zip, and buckle. Her large-motor development is also age-appropriate. She can jump rope, skip, hop, and jump. She has great balance and coordination.

Social-Emotional Development

Alyssa's social-emotional and work habits are also age-appropriate. She is respectful of others, follows directions, problem-solves with her peers, and separates from her parents easily. She is a confident and focused child.

Mathematical Concepts and Cognitive Development

Alyssa's mathematical skills and cognitive abilities show that she is ready for kindergarten. She can write and recognize all the upper- and lowercase letters, read several simple sight words, identify all the shapes she was shown, understand quantity, and count to 39.

General Comments

She is a confident and happy child who enjoys being in a learning environment. She appears ready for the new and exciting challenges that kindergarten will bring.

Sami's Summary

Motor Development

She has a great start to the development of her fine-motor skills. She holds a pencil correctly and can cut with ease. These skills are important to master before learning to print. Her large-motor skills are age-appropriate. She can run, gallop, ride a bike, and keep her body in her own personal space.

Social-Emotional Development

Sami is a happy girl who enjoys school and has positive self-esteem. She seldom has a hard time saying good-bye to mom, and has many friends. She is able to express feelings appropriately and verbally.

Mathematical Concepts and Cognitive Development

Sami's cognitive and mathematical understandings are age-appropriate. She still has some concepts to learn and discoveries to make before kindergarten. She was able to name most of the shapes asked and only became confused with one color. Even though she was unable to name any of the letters and numbers, she has great potential for doing so in the next year.

General Comments

Sami is a happy child who enjoys coming to school. She follows the classroom rules and respects peers and teachers. She will be successful getting ready for kindergarten during the year.

Observations of Alyssa and Sami (cont.)

Alyssa's Self-Portrait

Observations of Alyssa and Sami (cont.)

Sami's Self-Portrait

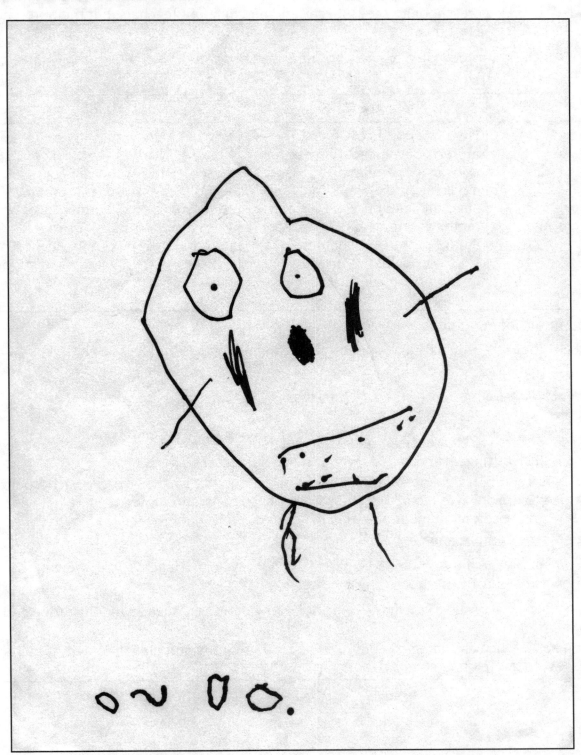

A Look at Two Preschool Children

Comparison of Alyssa and Sami

Alyssa and Sami were born on the same date, one year apart. When this assessment was done, Alyssa was five years, three months and Sami was four years, three months. The two girls have attended the same preschool for the last year, and had different teachers, but their preschool experiences have been similar.

This observation was designed to show how much a child can develop in all areas in just one year.

	Alyssa	Sami
Motor Development	Her fine- and gross-motor skills are well-developed. She uses scissors appropriately, holds a pencil correctly, and can snap, zip, and buckle. Her large motor development is also age-appropriate. She can jump rope, skip, hop, self-start on the swing, and jump. She has great balance and coordination.	She has a great start in developing her fine-motor skills. She holds a pencil correctly and can cut with ease. These skills are important to master before learning to print. Her large motor skills are age-appropriate. She can run, gallop, ride a bike, and keep her body in her own personal space.

Fine Motor Comparison

Both girls hold their pencils appropriately and can use scissors with ease.

- Alyssa was able to button, snap, and zip.
- Sami had a hard time with small focused tasks.

Self-Portrait

- Alyssa was able to create circles and insert small details such as ears. Alyssa also added details such as fingers and feet. Alyssa was also able to write her name.
- On Sami's self-portrait, she started her head at the top, but when she came back around she had to dip down to create the circle for her head. Sami attempted to write her name. She wrote the correct number of letters in her name, but they are illegible.

Large Motor Comparison

Both girls have age-appropriate large-motor skills. They are both active and energetic children who enjoy the outdoors.

- Alyssa has progressed to the more difficult large-motor tasks such as jumping rope and self-starting on the swing.
- Sami has all the basic large-motor skills mastered: running, jumping, hopping, galloping. She is also aware of personal space.

Comparison of Alyssa and Sami (cont.)

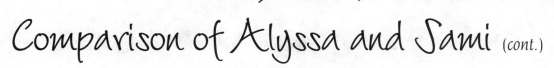

	Alyssa	Sami
Social-Emotional Development	Alyssa's social-emotional and work habits are also age-appropriate. She is respectful of others, follows directions; problem-solves with her peers, and separates from her parents easily. She is a confident and focused child.	Sami is a happy girl who enjoys school and has positive self-esteem. She seldom has a hard time saying good-bye to mom and has many friends. She is able to express feelings appropriately and verbally.

Social-Emotional Comparison

- Alyssa's social-emotional development is more advanced in the area of problem solving with peers and following three-step directions.
- Sami has not yet mastered the ability to problem-solve without adult supervision. She was able to follow two-step directions. Sami occasionally has some separation issues.
- Both children have excellent verbal abilities. They communicate easily with peers and are easy to understand.

Mathematical Concepts and Cognitive Development Comparison

- Alyssa's mathematical skills and cognitive abilities show that she is ready for kindergarten. She can write and recognize the entire set of upper- and lowercase letters, read several simple sight words, identify all the shapes she was shown, understand quantity, and count to 39.
- Alyssa recognizes all the upper- and lowercase letters of the alphabet. She can write them and sound out simple words.
- Alyssa was able to name the numerals 1 through 11 and could rote-count to 39.
- Sami's cognitive and mathematical understandings are age-appropriate. She still has some concepts to develop and discoveries to make before kindergarten. She was able to name most of the shapes that she was shown and only became confused identifying one color. Even though she was unable to name any of the letters and numbers, she has a great basis to expand in the next year.
- When Sami was tested on her knowledge of the alphabet, she was unable to name any letters. When she was asked to identify the letters, she would say letter names, but they didn't correspond with the letters she was being asked to name.
- Sami was unable to name any numerals, but she could count to 14.

Comparison

After reviewing both observations, each child is at her age-appropriate level and continues to develop appropriately. Children develop and grow at amazing rates in early childhood. A one-year difference may not seem much to adults, but in comparing young children, a year can make a huge developmental difference. A child can mature, increase his or her cognitive abilities, gain self-control, and develop a longer attention span in just one year. Sami is a happy and well-established four-year-old who has all the basic skills in all areas of development. In the next year, she will grow and fine-tune her skills in all areas of development. Alyssa is the typical five-year-old. She has mastered many of the skills necessary to help her become successful in kindergarten. In the next year, she will not only learn to add and subtract, but she will also learn to read.

Comparison of Alyssa and Sami (cont.)

Cutoff Dates for Kindergarten

In some states, the kindergarten cutoff date is as late as December 2, while some private schools have a cutoff date of July 1. These dates mean that the child must be five years old on or before that date to enter kindergarten. A child could start kindergarten in September at four, if his or her birthday falls before December 2. This means that a four-year-old could be in the same kindergarten class with a child who is about to turn six on December 3. There will also be children who start kindergarten at six years of age because the parents decided to wait a year before sending their child off to kindergarten. As you know from the comparison between Alyssa and Sami, one year can be a considerable difference.

Individually consider each child in all areas of development. Often, parents give their children the gift of time by allowing their child to stay in preschool one more year, even if the child's birthday would have allowed their child to go to kindergarten. Parents may choose to hold their child back for a variety of reasons, such as to allow more time to gain confidence and increase development before entering the formal school setting. If you have a child in your class who may not be ready for kindergarten, express those concerns to the parents and remember what a difference a year can make.

Developmentally Appropriate Practice

There are three main types of philosophies and approaches to educating young children.

Developmentally-Appropriate Practice

The Developmentally-Appropriate Practice is supported by the NAEYC (National Association for the Education of Young Children).

- This approach uses activities that are both age-appropriate and individually appropriate for each child.
- A developmentally-appropriate classroom will use curriculum that meets the needs of all children. For example, it is developmentally inappropriate to have a group of three-year-olds sitting at a table tracing letters on a worksheet. This is paper-and-pencil activity. If a three-year-old asks the teacher how to make the letter **M**, it is appropriate for the teacher to show the child, thus meeting the individual child's interests and needs.
  In a developmentally-appropriate preschool setting, you will see activities that are designed to develop positive self-esteem, social skills, cooperation, and problem-solving skills.
- There will be limited amounts of time during which the children are expected to sit, watch, and listen.

Montessori Approach

Maria Montessori created this method in the early 1900s.

- This method supports the natural development of children. When it came to learning, Montessori believed in turning to the child, observing the child, and following the child's lead.
- In a Montessori preschool, there will be large blocks of time with few interruptions during which the children are given the freedom to move from one activity to another.
- The materials will be hands-on and self-correcting. You will not find battery-operated toys in a Montessori classroom.

Reggio Emilia Philosophy

This method was developed by Reggio Emilia in Italy shortly after World War II.

- The curriculum in this type of classroom is planned by the children.
- Topics for study are taken from the children through talk and conversation.
- The teacher's role is to provide materials and to encourage small- and large-project work.
- Both the inside and outside areas are used as learning environments.

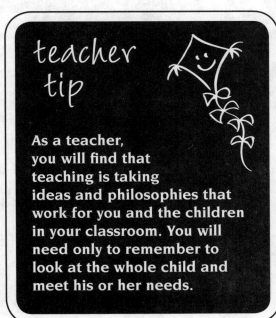

teacher tip

As a teacher, you will find that teaching is taking ideas and philosophies that work for you and the children in your classroom. You will need only to remember to look at the whole child and meet his or her needs.

Classroom Arrangement

When a parent or child enters your classroom, the environment should feel warm, comfortable, and safe. When establishing the feel for your classroom, think beyond room arrangement and remember to make it feel like a home. Children like and deserve to be surrounded by beauty and soft materials, and to feel safe. Your classroom should reflect the individual students and families instead of looking as if it were taken out of a catalog.

Classroom arrangement, organization, and the overall appearance need to be considered when setting up your classroom. These elements will help you maintain the environment children need in order to feel safe and be successful in your preschool class. An early childhood classroom should not feel sterile or look like an institution. Simple objects such as real plants, soft curtains, and walls painted in soft, warm, neutral colors will help create a soothing and homelike environment to which the children will respond.

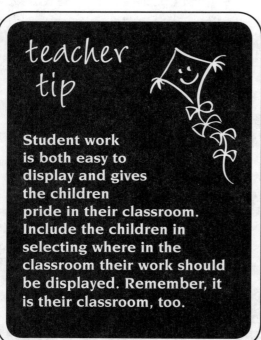

teacher tip

Student work is both easy to display and gives the children pride in their classroom. Include the children in selecting where in the classroom their work should be displayed. Remember, it is their classroom, too.

Educational elements in the surroundings should be visible, developmentally- and age-appropriate, and displayed in an aesthetically pleasing manner. Displaying the children's art and having a variety of decorations in the classroom are important; just be sure that you are not adding too much to the environment and overstimulating the children. The environment can and will have an effect on the children's behavior.

Often, parents will make a decision on a preschool by the feeling they get the first time they enter the classroom, so be prepared at all times for anyone to enter your class unannounced. You only get one chance to make a first impression. Be sure to take a few minutes to explain to parents the reasons for establishing your particular classroom environment. Help them understand that the environment sets the tone for how children function throughout the entire day.

Classroom Arrangement (cont.)

The classroom arrangement is essential in providing a safe environment for a child to learn and explore. The layout of the classroom must meet your needs as a teacher and the needs of all your students. Every item a child needs throughout the day should be within easy reach. A special-needs student should never be dependent upon another student or teacher to get something for him or her that is accessible to the rest of the class.

There are several things to consider when arranging a successful classroom: visibility, safety, small- and large-group areas, traffic patterns, active areas, quiet areas, and storage. When considering where to put work areas in the classroom, remember to include space for open-ended play and play areas that can be expanded without interrupting other work spaces.

As you begin looking at the room, available materials, and centers, make sure you have moveable furniture and quiet spaces.

- A portion of the shelving should be easy to move in order to expand certain areas. For example, blocks are heavy, so place them on a shelf that is on wheels and can be moved to make more space for a structure or for a large train track. This will quickly allow the children to further expand their play.
- You also want to have places where a child can be alone. By hanging transparent fabric to separate areas, you will create a comfortable environment in which a child may do a quiet activity.

teacher tip

Keep in mind any students you may have who have special needs. Children with walkers or wheelchairs need more space between shelving to be able to move easily through the environment.

Visibility

Visibility in the Classroom

When determining furniture arrangement, keep in mind that each child must be within sight and sound of you at all times. Never put your back to the class. You are responsible for monitoring what is happening in the entire classroom. When two adults are working in a classroom, one can focus on a small group while the other observes the rest of the students. For example, one teacher can sit on the floor to play a game with a small group of students. A second teacher or teaching assistant can keep an eye on the other students around the room. Below are some suggestions for maximizing visibility in the classroom.

- Position tall shelves and cubbies against the wall. For area dividers, use shorter shelves over which the teacher can see while sitting at a table.
- Place fish-eye mirrors like those found in stores in the upper corners of the room. This will also help you see what may be going on in a blind spot in the classroom or behind furniture.
- Establish a teacher-directed or small-group area so the entire room is visible. For example, a circular table can be used for an activity requiring the teacher to practice writing with the children. Sit on the far side of the table with your back to the wall so the rest of the class is still visible.

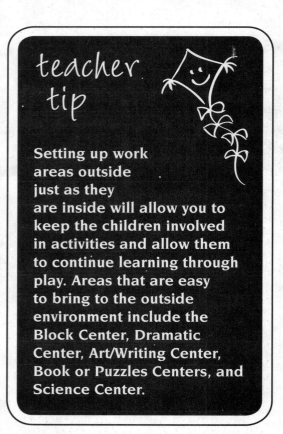

teacher tip

Setting up work areas outside just as they are inside will allow you to keep the children involved in activities and allow them to continue learning through play. Areas that are easy to bring to the outside environment include the Block Center, Dramatic Center, Art/Writing Center, Book or Puzzles Centers, and Science Center.

Visibility Outside

The same principles of visibility should be applied to the outside area. When dealing with children, accidents will naturally occur because children playing outside are using their large-motor skills, which may not yet be developed, and are more willing to take risks. If a child is hurt or there is an accident, it is your responsibility to see what happened. Never put your back to a group of children unless you know another teacher is watching that area. The playground is a difficult area to monitor. The children are constantly moving around a large outdoor area. As a teacher, you need to keep moving and keep your eyes and ears open. If children are getting hurt or seem to be getting into trouble outside, you may want to evaluate whether there are enough appropriate things for the children to do or if the adult-to-child ratio is adequate.

Safety

Providing a clean and safe environment for all the children in your class is one of your top priorities.

Cleaning

Most schools have an evening cleaning crew to clean the classrooms. Make sure that your cleaning crew regularly does the following tasks:

- Wipe off all tables, countertops, and sink with paper towels and cleaner.
- Vacuum the carpet area.
- Empty the trash cans.
- Mop the floors.
- Clean the bathroom (toilet and sink).
- Refill any daily products (paper towels, toilet paper, plastic gloves).
- Clean ceiling fans, mirrors, windows, and walls.
- Professionally clean the carpet and clean and rewax the floors at least twice a year.

General Safety Tips

All classroom items, furniture, rugs, and equipment need to be in good working order and made child-proof. Here is a checklist to help with furniture safety.

- The shelves in the class should be smooth and free of nails and screws.
- Tables and chairs should be at the children's height so that they can easily get in and out of them.
- Soft furniture, such as sofas and beanbags, must be easy to clean and free from strings or loose buttons.
- Do not place any shelving in front of an exit.
- Have the emergency evacuation plan posted next to every door.
- The cords to all window blinds need to be tied up and out of the children's reach.
- Outlets must have safety caps.
- Cleaning materials must be stored in an upper cabinet with locks or in a storage room.
- Do not allow any adult to have a hot beverage in your class.
- Store your personal items, such as your purse, in an upper cabinet or locked cupboard.

teacher tip

Avoid using sponges. They are a perfect place for mold and germs to grow. Use paper towels as much as possible.

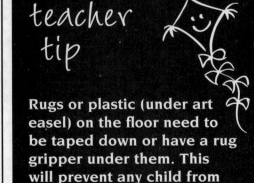

teacher tip

Rugs or plastic (under art easel) on the floor need to be taped down or have a rug gripper under them. This will prevent any child from tripping on a corner or having the rug shift under him or her.

Safety *(cont.)*

Toys

The task toys and equipment will get lots of use. Each week when you sanitize and rotate the task toys, inspect each piece to make sure that all toys are in good working condition. Any broken or damaged toys need to be thrown away. Parents should never see a broken or cracked toy. This is true for outside toys as well.

Sanitizing Toys

When sanitizing the toys in your class, do not try to clean all the toys in your classroom in one day. It will take up too much of your time taking them all out and putting them away. Instead, the closing teacher should sanitize the toys from a different area of the classroom when school is over.

- Allow the toys to air-dry overnight.
- The opening teacher puts away the newly cleaned toys.

If you see a child put a toy in his or her mouth, simply ask that child to either place the toy in the teacher sink to be washed by you, or ask the child to go to the sink and wash the toy with soap and water. You can always use a spray disinfectant for items that cannot be placed in a sink to be washed, like door handles or wooden blocks. The areas in the classroom that will need to be sanitized the most often are:

- Dramatic Play Center
- Task Center
- Sensory Center
- Block Center (in the Block Center, you will need to clean all plastic accessories not the wooden blocks)

teacher tip

Use two tablespoons of bleach to one gallon of water to sanitize your toys.

Safety (cont.)

Communication

Teacher communication is also essential for maintaining a safe environment.

- Never assume that the other teacher or teacher's aide knows what you are doing or where you are going. For example, if you need to assist a child in the restroom, tell the other adult where you are going, why you are going, and about how long you will be. For example, "Mrs. Smith, Jack had an accident, so I am going to help him in the bathroom. I will try to be back in five minutes." This will let the other teacher know that the children in the class are now his or her sole responsibility.
- Never leave another teacher in the room if it will make your classroom out of compliance with the state or the school's student-teacher ratio requirement. If you need to leave the room and no other adult can come into the class to assist the other teacher in maintaining the student-teacher ratio, take more than one child with you.

Again, be prepared for anyone to enter the classroom unannounced, including the director, a licensing inspector, or a parent.

Emergencies

Living in today's world, you need to be prepared for anything that may happen. If an earthquake hit today, would you and your class be able to survive for two days without help? In case of an emergency, either natural or community, you need to be prepared. Have enough supplies on hand to last you and your students for one to two days without outside assistance.

Natural Emergency

A natural emergency is something that occurs in the environment, such as an earthquake, storm, fire, or tornado. These can be devastating and can happen with minimal or no warning. First, you need to practice drills with your class. Teach them how to duck and cover, leave the building, and to remain calm.

Community Emergency

A community emergency is something that happens in the neighborhood or area surrounding the school, such as a plane crash, a bomb threat, or a terrorist attack. Your school should have an emergency plan in place in case of a community emergency.

Safety (cont.)

Emergency Supplies

If you need to evacuate the classroom, you need to have a prepacked bag or backpack that you can take with you. If you and the children are barricaded in the classroom, you will need a large tub to hold necessary materials to survive a few days without help.

teacher tip

Use a brightly colored (red or orange) bag or backpack labeled **EMERGENCY** to hold your emergency supplies, and have it hanging next to the door.

The emergency bag should contain the following items:		
Adhesive tape	Cotton balls	Large adhesive pads
Band-Aids	Q-Tips	Flashlight
Safety pins	Sterile gloves	Pens and paper
Gauze bandage roll	Cold compress	Small scissors
Bacterial wipes	Batteries	Tissue
Felt pen	Petroleum jelly	Lollipops
Book and art supplies	Whistle	Copies of the children's emergency numbers

The classroom tub should have the following items:		
Dust masks	Liquid soap	Coffee can
Toilet paper	Work gloves	Crow bar
Aluminum foil	Masking tape	Paper towels
Two sponges	Adult outfit	Plastic trash bags
Duct tape	Drinking cups	Granola bars
Raisins	Juice boxes	Drinking water

Group Areas

Every activity in an early childhood classroom has purpose, whether it is a small, intimate experience with a group of four to six children, an activity with the entire group, individual choice, or work time. The environment needs to be adaptable to the activity and the purpose. Arranging the class while allowing space for both large and small groups needs to be one of your priorities.

Small Group

A small-group activity:

- is a teacher-directed activity.
- has six or fewer children in the group.
- has a specific result in mind.

Small group is a time to introduce science or math concepts and language development activities.

- The area you choose for a small group activity should be a consistent spot in the classroom. This will eliminate any confusion for the children.
- A good spot for a small group activity is either at a table where other activities in the class will not be a distraction, or a section on the rug that still allows you to observe the rest of the students working in other areas.
- If you have a teacher's aide, you will be able to break up the class into two smaller groups.
- Have each group work on different concepts for a short time—15 minutes for example—and then switch with the other teacher.
- This allows the teachers to introduce two different concepts to the children, provide each child with individual attention, and focus on the activity at hand without having to keep an eye on any other children who may be working in the classroom.

Large Group

A large-group activity includes everyone in the class.

- The area you allow for large groups in your classroom needs to accommodate each child so that he or she has enough personal space to feel comfortable.
- The area in which you choose to put the large-group area needs to be free from distractions.
- Giving the children a specific spot, such as a piece of carpet, a hot pad, or a magazine covered in material with either their names or a symbol on it, will eliminate some of the confusion and arguments as to who gets to sit next to whom.
- This also allows you to separate children who may be distracting one another. The children need to be able to focus on you and the activity.

Large-group or circle time activities are:

- Read-aloud times
- Calendar
- Other informal activities
- Announcements
- Music and movement

Traffic Patterns

The traffic pattern you create for you classroom will either foster harmony or cause chaos. A good classroom arrangement will allow a child to walk from one area of the classroom to another area without disrupting the other children.

Moving from One Area to Another

During work time, the children should be able to function on their own. Rearranging furniture several times to place it in spots that will work is acceptable, and often necessary. Include the children in helping you plan where the furniture will go, and have them help rearrange the class. Look for areas that are too close together, too big or too open, and straight paths from one end of the room to another.

What to Avoid

Ask yourself, "When a child is moving from one area to another, does he or she have to go through one area or several other areas to get where he or she needs to go?" If this is the case, something needs to change. The last thing a teacher or child wants is problems during work time.

- For example, if Sami and Melissa are building a tower in Block Area and Tom has to walk through the blocks to get to the Art Area, there is a potential for problems. Tom may accidentally knock over Sami and Melissa's tower, causing hurt feelings, finger pointing, and the possibility of someone getting hit by a falling block.
- If there is a straight path in the classroom, the children will use it as an avenue for running.
- Ensure that you have adequate space near doors to line up the students prior to leaving the classroom.
- Plan for emergencies by having exits clear and accessible at all points in the day. Think about what will occur in each area throughout the day. For example, the blocks may be stored neatly under a cabinet, but be sure that students would not be blocking an exit when playing with the blocks.

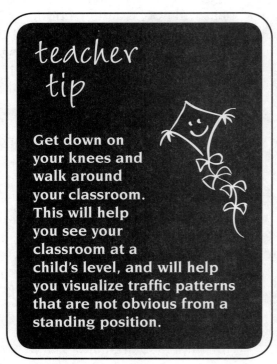

teacher tip

Get down on your knees and walk around your classroom. This will help you see your classroom at a child's level, and will help you visualize traffic patterns that are not obvious from a standing position.

Active and Quiet Areas

Providing both active and quiet areas in the class will allow the child to choose the type of activity he or she is interested in and that will meet his or her needs at that given time. Having a balance of both types of play or work space will give each child the opportunity to go from an active area to a quiet area when feeling overstimulated. A good classroom has a balance of quiet and active areas. Active and quiet areas need to be on opposite ends of the room.

Active Areas

Areas in which the child is moving his or her entire body are considered active areas. Active areas often get loud and can be distracting. Examples of active areas: Block Area, Music and Movement Center, Dramatic Center, and Sensory Center.

Quiet Areas

Quiet areas are places in the classroom where a child can do an activity with one friend or alone.

- A child may need a quiet, comfortable space to be alone and retreat from all the stimulation that is happening in the class.
- Quiet areas provide that sanctuary, as well as a place for a downtime in the class.
- Don't underestimate the need for a child to be alone or have some downtime. This time allows a child to restore energy or think quietly before returning to the regular classroom activity.
- Provide soft materials such as pillows, stuffed animals, or blankets.
- You can create an intimate space by hanging see-through netting from the ceiling. The children will feel some sense of privacy, yet they are still visible.
- Examples of quiet areas include: the Book Center, Listening Center, Art/Writing Center, Task Center, and Science Center.

Arranging Furniture for Expanded Play

Allow the children to be flexible in how they use the materials in the classroom. Let the children take materials from one work area to another. Books do not have to stay in the Book Center. The child may take a book to Block Center to compare the pictures of the trucks in the book with the trucks in Block Center. Support the children in expanded play and avoid rules that are not necessary.

- A child is working in Block Center building a house with large hollow blocks. The child may want to use blankets, pillows, or play food to extend his or her play, and these items are found in the Dramatic Play Center. Placing Block Center close to the Dramatic Play Center will encourage continuous expanded play.
- Other areas to consider putting near each other are the Art/Writing Center and the Dramatic Play Center. These two areas complement each other by allowing children to make menus, pictures, and other written props for role-playing.
- Placing the Book Center and Listening Center next to Art/Writing Center allows the children to create and imitate what they are being exposed to in books.

Storage

Storage is often a problem in preschool classrooms. There never seems to be enough of it. Keeping things organized will:

- help you find items when they are needed.
- allow you to rotate your toys.
- help give you more storage space.

Storing Manipulative or Task Toys

- Keep all the toys you want to rotate in see-through plastic containers with lids.
- Label each container by sticking the name and picture of the items on the outside of the box with clear packing tape.
- Keep all the manipulatives you are rotating in the same-size container. This will help keep the cupboard organized and make it easy to rotate the toys. As you begin to rotate the toys, pull the new manipulatives that the students will work with off the shelf and replace them with the container holding the manipulatives they had been using.
- Remember, when putting the rotated toys back into the cupboard, to sanitize them and put the box at the bottom of the shelf under toys the children have yet to work with. This will allow you to simply grab the top box and not have to worry about the last time the children had the manipulative available.
- Labeling each shelf in the cupboard will allow you to put items where they belong.
- Labeling a shelf just for puzzles, manipulatives, books, math counters, writing, games, etc., will remind you, your aide, or a substitute where to return items so they can easily be found again when needed. Having everything labeled takes a lot of effort at first but will save you time and keep you organized in the long run.

Storing Paper

You can make your own construction paper rack by purchasing pieces of thin wood at the local hardware store, cut specifically to fit into one of the cupboards. You can stack the different-colored construction paper by color.

- Find a cupboard that will fit the construction paper lying flat.
- Decide how many colors you would like to keep in the classroom. Some teachers like to have all the colors available, and some may like to keep only the primary colors plus black and white. If you are going to keep six different colors in the class, you will need five pieces of wood.
- Next, measure the cupboard. Remember to measure the inside of the cupboard and make it a half-inch smaller on each side. This will ensure that the wood will fit inside the cupboard. five pieces of wood.
- The next step is to take a block from Block Area (the small rectanglular ones work well) and place one block on each side and the back of the shelf. Place the cut piece of thin wood on top. Again, place a block on each side and on the back of the thin wood, and put the next piece of thin wood on top of the second set of blocks. Keep going until you have a homemade shelf that will hold the construction paper and keep it organized.

Storage (cont.)

Storing Art Materials

Art materials such as bottles of paint, paintbrushes, watercolors, collage materials, miscellaneous painting items, and glue should be stored together.

- Creating a central location will help you or the children find items when needed.
- Children enjoy helping, being part of a class, and having responsibilities. Giving a couple of children the "job" of getting art ready will not only help you but will also allow the children to feel useful and to practice following directions.
- When having the students help, be specific on what you would like put on the table. For example, "Matt and Sophia, for our art activity today, we need four bottles of glue, the feathers, the yarn, and pompons put on the table."
- Placing the art items in a lower cupboard will allow easy access for the children. When the children get involved in an art activity, they will think of something else that they need for their collage or art project. Just require them to ask you before getting something additional out of the art cupboard so you don't end up with everything on the art table at once.
- Keep one bottle of each paint color in the classroom. This will save time by not having to go to the storeroom every day.
- Use plastic boxes or shoeboxes for keeping supplies of collage materials, watercolors, and a variety of things in the cupboard for painting. Because shoeboxes are not see-through, place a picture and a word describing what is inside on the outside of the boxes so a child can easily find what he or she may need.
- Keep the paintbrushes sorted by size in plastic cups, with the bristles up. Storing the different-size paintbrushes separately will allow a child to grab the size needed and not have to dig through a cup to find it.
- Keeping construction paper in the classroom can take up a lot of space and can become messy. However, if you have room, it is an excellent idea to keep as much in the classroom as possible.

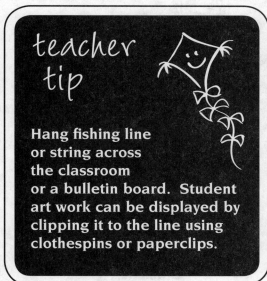

teacher tip

Hang fishing line or string across the classroom or a bulletin board. Student art work can be displayed by clipping it to the line using clothespins or paperclips.

Sample Floor Plans — Layout #1

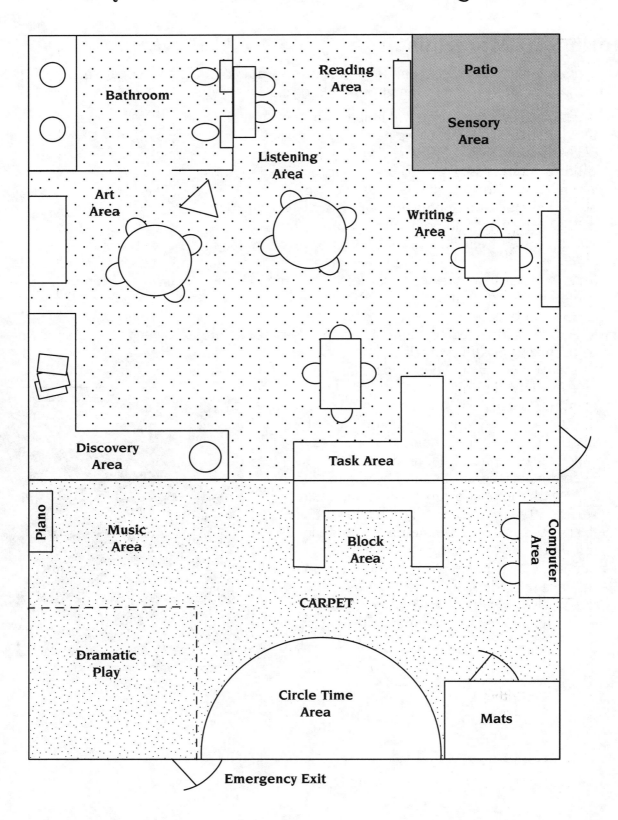

Sample Floor Plans — Layout #2

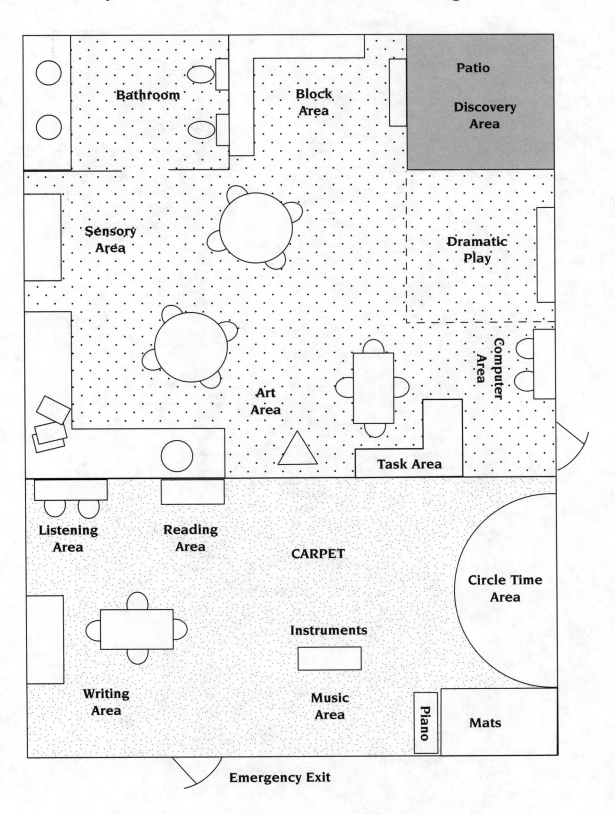

Bathroom

Block Area

Patio

Discovery Area

Sensory Area

Dramatic Play

Computer Area

Art Area

Task Area

Listening Area

Reading Area

CARPET

Circle Time Area

Instruments

Writing Area

Music Area

Piano

Mats

Emergency Exit

Sample Floor Plans — Layout #3

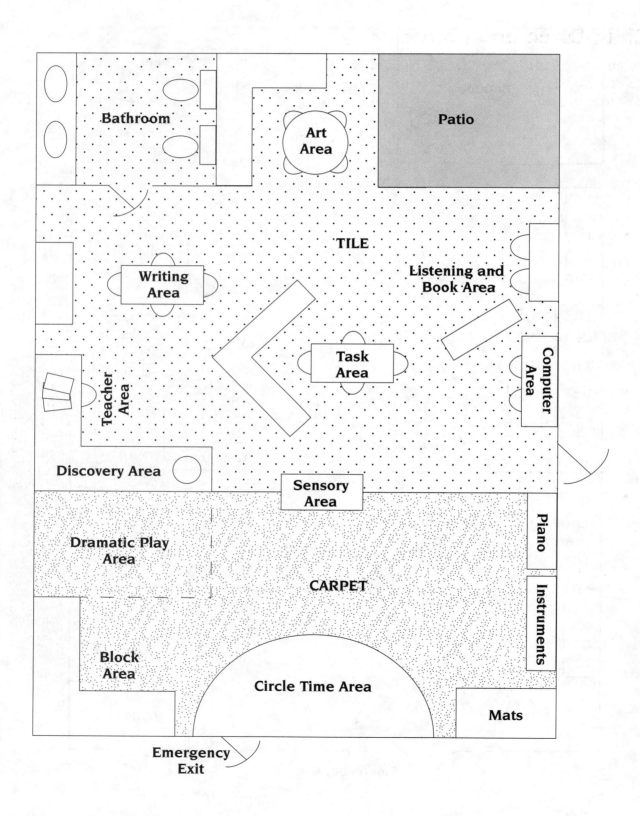

Organization

Child-Directed Centers

Organizing child-directed centers, take-home projects, and teacher items will help your classroom stay clean and will help you to quickly find items you need. Child-directed centers are areas the children choose to work at during open play time or work time. Child-directed centers are:

- Blocks
- Task
- Science
- Reading or Book
- Science
- Listening
- Dramatic Play
- Art/Writing
- Sensory
- Computer
- Music and Movement

Create an organized space. By the first day of class, label each shelf, container, and area with both word(s) and picture. By doing this, you will not have to answer the question "Where does this go?" at cleanup time.

Blocks Center

Organizing the Blocks Center

- First, empty out all the blocks on to the floor.
- Decide where the different shapes will best fit on the shelves. Place long, flat rectanglular blocks on the bottom and put similar shapes close together or on the same shelf. Put all the blocks away, making sure they all fit neatly.
- Trace one block from each group on the same color piece of construction paper, to create an outline of the block, and cut it out.
- Tape down the silhouette on the shelf with clear packing tape or contact paper in front of the shelf where the blocks are to be put away. The child can lay a block on the construction paper to see if the shapes match. This is a great way to help the children with geometric shapes and matching, as well as teaching them how to keep the area neat.

teacher tip

Obtain a duplicate copy of the catalog from which you order materials. Keep one with your files for future orders. Cut the picture of what you ordered out of the other to use as your picture label.

Organization (cont.)

Dramatic Play Center

Organizing the Dramatic Play Center is easy. Start with the kitchen.

- Find all the play food. Find a container that will hold all the food. Label the container with the word *food* and a picture. Put the container on the refrigerator shelf that has the same food picture that is on the outside of the container. The children can match the picture or word.
- Next, find a container that will hold all the dishes and label it in the same way that you did with the food. You may want to break down the food and dishes into categories, such as plates, cups, and utensils, but this takes more containers and space.
- Next, find a space, either a dresser or rack that will hold all the hats, clothes, and shoes. Again, label each drawer or rack with both the word and picture.

Task Center

Task Center should have at least five different small motor toys for the children to choose from.

- These manipulatives should be rotated often and kept in same-size clear containers.
- This will allow for a quick rotation and help the area look and remain organized.
- Puzzles may also be part of this area. Puzzle racks are an excellent way to keep the puzzles organized.
- Label the shelf in front of the rack with the word *puzzles* and a picture.

Art/Writing Center

It is appropriate to combine the art and writing into one area in the classroom.

- For young children, pictures are the way in which they begin to tell stories. This area will need to have lots of materials available for the students to create.
- Each item, from large items like easels to small items like scissors, needs to have a specific spot in the area.
- Label everything with the word and a picture.

teacher tip

Placing a foldable sandwich bag in the art easel paint cups will allow easy clean up. Simply throw the bag away and replace it with a new bag and paint color.

Organization (cont.)

Discovery Center

- Discovery or Sensory Center is an area in which a child can explore different textures and materials. Put reusable items (sand, dry beans, cotton balls, noodles, and dirt) in large plastic containers with lids—for example, large mayonnaise containers found at wholesale stores. Plastic containers can be written on with markers and are safe to have around children. These can be kept in a cupboard or under your sensory bin.
- When you use water in your sensory bin, replace it each day.
- Other materials that should not be reused are flour, salt, cornstarch, and anything else that may attract bugs.
- At the end of the week when the children are done, either throw the sensory material into the trash or place them in an airtight container.

Reading or Book Center

Reading or Book Area can be organized by having a spinning book rack or a book rack that is flat against the wall.

- Put out only enough books to fill the rack neatly. Overfilling will cause the children to cram the books, and some may get destroyed.
- Small baskets may also be used. Have a separate basket for board books, magazines, books related to a theme, or newspapers.
- If you choose to use baskets or bins, label them so the children will know where to return the reading materials.
- Give the children different materials to read in order to become familiar with print.

teacher tip

By hanging a transparent curtain around this area, you will create a quiet and private area for the children to read.

Computer Center

Organizing the Computer Center is easy.

- The computer, keyboard, mouse, and timer should be the only items on the desk or small table. This is one area in the classroom that the teacher controls.
- Put a different game in the computer each day. Explain the game of the day and do not change it. This will encourage the students to try new games and not always play his or her favorite one.
- Keep the computer games in the teacher cupboard away from access of the children.
- Some of the children will be more computer-literate than others, and even you, and can figure out how to change the game and many other settings on the computer. Be aware of what is going on in this area during work time.

Organization (cont.)

Science Area

In your Science Center, you will have materials that will stay out year-round such as plants or classroom pets. Other objects in this area need to be rotated.

- Keep your science items by theme in plastic containers.
- For example, all materials relating to the human body are kept together and all the magnets are kept together.
- This will allow you to pull a container when looking for something and not have to dig around.

Music and Movement Area

- Each musical instrument should have a safe place in which to be put away at cleanup time.
- Plastic containers or a musical instrument rack are the best places to keep the instruments from getting broken.
- Keep a variety of musical instruments in a special place just for circle or large-group time. This will make these instruments special.

Listening Center

Listening Center is where a child can choose to listen to a story on tape or CD while following along with the book.

- Placing the story and tape or CD in a plastic hanging bag or in a recloseable bag allows the children to be completely independent.
- All the children will need to do is to select the story and place the tape in the tape player. They will not be relying on you to find the tape that corresponds to the book.

teacher tip

Headphones are a great addition to the Listening Center. They keep the children's attention and allow the children to listen to a story with minimal outside noise.

Organization (cont.)

Take-Home Projects

Every parent enjoys seeing what his or her child created. One way to store take-home projects is using a legal-size file folder box. Put a hanging folder, one for each child in the class, into the file box. Label the outside with either "Take-Home Projects" or "Our Art." Encourage parents to collect their child's art weekly.

Teacher-Only Materials

- Other teacher materials, such as circle-time books and curriculum materials, should be stored on their own shelves or in a separate cupboard.
- Keep the children's personal information, such as emergency numbers and parent information, behavior notes, and sick days, in a file box, notebook, or folder away from access of others.

Children's Portfolios

Keeping a cumulative portfolio to show or give to the parents at parent-teacher conferences is an excellent way to show improvement.

- Use a separate folder box for each child. Keep it separate from the take-home projects file box so that parents will not get confused.
- A great way to start the portfolio during the first days of class is to have each child write his or her name, cut and draw a picture of himself or herself, and date the samples. Place these examples in the child's portfolio.
- Put something into the portfolio about every two to three weeks (samples of cutting, writing, creative art) with the date it was created.
- When the child constructs something that he or she is extremely proud of or you think is a wonderful example of creativity, put it into the portfolio.

Parents will be delighted to have concrete examples of the improvement their child is making in class.

Large Teacher Bulletin Board Items

Teacher materials such as large posters and bulletin board materials can be stored in large folders.

- Take two pieces of cardboard that have been taped on the sides and bottom, creating a large folder, and store them upright.
- Label the cardboard folders with what is inside them. This will eliminate you having to look through all the folders to find what you need.
- Make four large cardboard folders, one for each season, to store seasonal materials.

Because the folders are flat, they may be stored right behind shelves that may be up against the wall, or you can purchase rectanglular cardboard boxes to store the folders.

Bulletin Boards

Bulletin boards in the class can be used for many different purposes. They can be used for displaying:

- student art
- information related to a theme
- pictures of families
- things found in the environment
- professional art

Bulletin boards should be changed at least once a month.

Displaying Children's Artwork

Children like to see their accomplishments on display, and displaying the children's artwork is a way of validating what the children have created. When displaying the students' art, be respectful. Do not just throw it up on the bulletin board with a simple staple. Place a colored piece of paper behind it, creating a frame. Having one bulletin board designated for creative art is an excellent way of rotating artwork. If a child wants a new piece of his or her art displayed, it needs to replace the one that is already up.

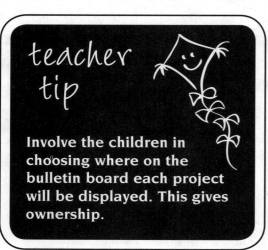

teacher tip

Involve the children in choosing where on the bulletin board each project will be displayed. This gives ownership.

Monthly Themes

Bulletin boards are also a way to display information related to the monthly theme. If the children are learning about insects, put up lots of pictures of ants, caterpillars, butterflies, bees, and grasshoppers. This will create interest within the children and encourage the children to discuss what they see in the picture.

Professional Art

Bringing in pieces of art made by famous artists, such as Pablo Picasso's *Three Musicians*, Leonardo da Vinci's *Mona Lisa*, Claude Monet's *Lily Pond*, Vincent van Gogh's *The Starry Night*, Andy Warhol's *Campbell's Soup Can*, and Georgia O'Keeffe's *Lake George, Early Moonrise Spring* can add to the aesthetically pleasing atmosphere of the classroom and help develop an appreciation for the fine arts. These masterpieces can be purchased at the local poster store and are relatively inexpensive if not purchased in a frame. You may want to laminate the posters before displaying them in your classroom. Rotating these pieces of art is a good way to encourage the children to look at the artwork and try to figure out what materials the artist used and how the artist created the picture.

Bulletin Boards (cont.)

Family Photos and "Star of the Week"

At the beginning of the school year when the theme is "All About Me," have the children bring in pictures of their families. This will allow the children to talk with one another about their families and to bring their home lives to school. Often, it is comforting for a child to see pictures of the people he or she misses during the day. You can also pick a child each week to be the "Star of the Week." This child can bring in pictures of his or her family. (See page 50 for a Star of the Week Questionnaire that can used on a bulletin board.)

Things Found in the Child's Environment

Having bulletin boards in the different areas in your classroom allows you to display pictures of items that the children will see in the environment. For example, in the Dramatic Play Center, place pictures of families engaged in activities together: eating dinner, cooking, playing at the park, or reading stories; or use community helpers. In the Block Area, you can display pictures of different buildings and forms of transportation. Additionally, encourage the children to bring words from their environments that they are able to read. Cut out the front of a box of cereal, advertisements from the paper, or pictures of street signs. Young children will recognize many of these words from the environment and "read" them.

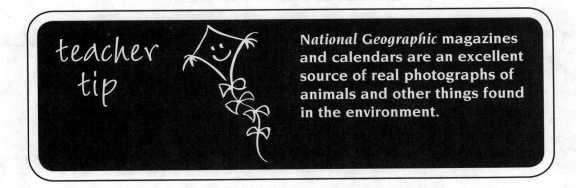

teacher tip

National Geographic magazines and calendars are an excellent source of real photographs of animals and other things found in the environment.

Bulletin Boards (cont.)

This is to be filled out by the child and parents.

Title: Star of the Week is _____

(picture of the child)

I am _____ years old.

My dad and mom's names are _____

My sister's name is _____

My brother's name is _____

My pets and their names are _____

My favorite food is _____

My favorite book is _____

My favorite color is _____

My favorite toy is _____

I have the most fun when I am _____

Classroom Setup Conclusion

Some questions to ask yourself when arranging your classroom:

- How am I going to use the shelving in the room?

- Do I have enough different areas and centers for all the children in the class to be working in at the same time?

- Does each child have enough personal space at Circle Time?

- Is Circle Time sheltered from outside distractions?

- Do I have a specific spot for Small-Group Time?

- When sitting at a table, can I still see what is happening in the rest of the classroom?

- When the children are in class, how will they move from one area to another?

- If a child needs help, do I have a plan that requires me to leave the classroom?

- When I need to find a manipulative, book, or puzzle do I know where to look?

- Are the toys that will rotate labeled and readily available to the children?

- Can each student in the class function independently and not need help from me to get materials?

- How will a child with special needs function in the class?

- Are active areas separated from the quiet areas in the class?

- Do I allow for work areas to overlap for more creative and extended play?

- Do I provide a quiet space for a child who may be overstimulated or wants to be alone?

- Are teacher materials stored separately from materials for the students?

- Are materials stored together according to use?

- Are materials organized and in containers?

- If I were a substitute, would I know where to find things?

- Can children independently put work and art items away at cleanup time?

- Are the Art/Writing Center and Sensory Center close to a sink?

- Is the room clean and uncluttered?

Centers

As an early childhood teacher, it is your responsibility to attend to the whole child: the social, emotional, cognitive, and physical development of each of your students. Provide many age- and developmentally-appropriate materials in your classroom environment.

Dividing your classroom into organized and well-defined areas of interest or centers is essential in providing opportunities for developing logical-thinking skills, reflecting on the environment, and allowing the children opportunities for exploratory play.

- During work time or center time, the children should be able to function independently and require minimum teacher direction. You should be able to play with the children, listen to their conversations, and have fun with them.

- Each child in your class will have different interests, be on different levels, and learn at different rates. By providing opportunities for active play and hands-on activities in the different centers, you will meet the needs of all your students.

- Centers allow children to manipulate objects, engage in pretend play, develop their language, experiement, and problem-solve.

- Centers allow children to develop and use both small- and large-motor skills.

- Provide realistic concrete materials and keep the centers open to natural play that is comfortable, easy to understand, and positively directed.

- Emphasize the success and creativity in each child. This will give them the confidence to try new things without fear of failure.

- Work time and center time are the most valuable elements in the early childhood classroom. They allow the children to make choices, experiment, and learn about themselves and the world around them.

- Centers are the core of the early childhood classroom. The possibility for centers and creative learning are limitless. The activities in each of the following centers should contain self-correcting and self-directed activities.

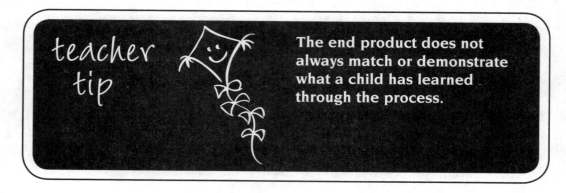

teacher tip

The end product does not always match or demonstrate what a child has learned through the process.

Task Center

Task Center, sometimes called the Math Center or Manipulative Center, encourages children's understanding of mathematical concepts. A child not only begins to understand complex mathematical concepts, but these activities also require the use of the small-motor skills by counting, classifying, ordering, and measuring.

The children working in this center will increase their cognitive development as they estimate, develop one-to-one correspondence, make comparisons, and manipulate objects.

Materials

Manipulatives often have limited possibilities for creative and divergent play. Provide both a table with chairs and a rug area so the children can choose where they would like to work. Some children prefer to sit at a table while others may choose to sit on the floor, allowing for more room and expanded play.

Some typical materials in this area include:

Board games	Simple card games	Geo boards
Pegboards	Lacing cards and lacing beads	Puzzles
Other structured materials		

Storage

The materials for the Task Center need to be stored in low, open shelves in plastic buckets or containers labeled with the word and picture to assist children in keeping the center organized.

teacher tip

Keep in mind that some of the objects found in Task Center may be considered "Chokeable Items" and should be used only by older children.

Location in the Classroom

Task Center can be placed in between the quiet and active areas. The children working in this center will be able to concentrate enough to finish a task without being distracted by the active loud areas like the Block Center and Dramatic Play Center. Yet these children will probably be quiet enough so as to not be a distraction to the children who have chosen to work on a quiet activity. This is an excellent buffer between active and quiet areas.

Task Center (cont.)

Task Center Checklist

- ❏ geoboards
- ❏ pegboards
- ❏ lacing cards
- ❏ lacing beads and strings
- ❏ puzzles
- ❏ hammer and golf tees with foam board
- ❏ interlocking plastic and wooden sets or toys
- ❏ nuts and bolts
- ❏ variety of bottles and tops for matching
- ❏ board games
- ❏ card games
- ❏ stacking toys
- ❏ toys that can be taken apart and put back together
- ❏ large shape and color sorters
- ❏ magnetic board with letters and shapes
- ❏ abacus
- ❏ balances
- ❏ dominoes
- ❏ scales

Dramatic Play Center

The Dramatic Play Center (sometimes also called the Pretend Center, Make-Believe Center, or Fantasy Center) offers a safe environment for children to:

- Develop language
- Test social skills
- Act out situations
- Explore different occupations
- Explore different social roles and behaviors
- Develop an understanding of how the world works
- Express feelings
- Be exposed to different cultures

By observing the children playing in this center, you can gain insight into the children's backgrounds, experiences, and developmental needs. Activities in this area also promote hand/eye coordination and small-muscle development.

Prop Boxes

Rotating or adding new objects to this area is easy if you have prop boxes available. A prop box is a kit that contains a collection of real objects that relate to the same theme. For example, a pizza parlor prop box could contain aprons, a chef's hat, menus, pizza boxes, pizza pans, a serving tray, cups, a pitcher, silverware, play money, a cash register, pencils, and order pads. By storing all the contents in a prop box, you can change your Dramatic Play Center quickly and provide opportunities for extended play. Listed below are other suggestions for prop boxes.

- Birthday Party
- Gas Station
- Picnic
- Ice Cream Shop
- Doctor's Office
- Library
- Beauty Shop
- Pet Care
- Dance
- Cowboys & Cowgirls
- Camping
- Safari

teacher tip

Stock the Dramatic Play Center with environmental print items that relate to the theme of the prop box. Empty cereal boxes, old phone books, or restaurant menus are excellent sources of print for the children to explore in this center.

Dramatic Play Center (cont.)

Materials

Some of the things in this center become permanent elements (for example, a play kitchen). Providing real materials, such as pots and pans, an iron, and a blow dryer (with the cords cut off), promotes Dramatic Play Center experiences and expands the interest of the children. Adult-size clothing and shoes can be purchased at garage sales and thrift stores, or you can ask parents for donations.

Storage

Items in this area should be stored in logical places where a child might find the objects at home. Play food should be stored in the refrigerator, the dishes stored in a play cupboard, dress-up clothing can be placed in a dresser. Promote literacy and organizational skills by labeling each item with the word and a corresponding picture.

Changing the Area

The Dramatic Play Center can be altered to incorporate a thematic unit. For example, if the theme of the class is Valentine's Day and community helpers, the dramatic play care can be transformed into a post office by adding a mailbox, mail carrier bag, envelopes, scales, stamp pads, and a mail carrier uniform. The Dramatic Play Center includes an assortment of fantasy play equipment.

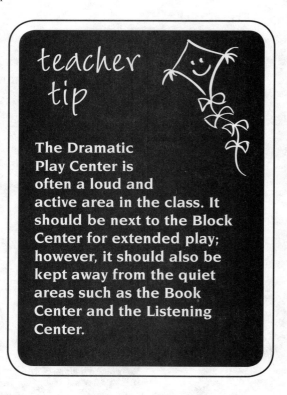

teacher tip

The Dramatic Play Center is often a loud and active area in the class. It should be next to the Block Center for extended play; however, it should also be kept away from the quiet areas such as the Book Center and the Listening Center.

Dramatic Play Center (cont.)

Dramatic Play Center Checklist

- ❏ child-size play kitchen (sink, stove, cupboard, and refrigerator)

- ❏ variety of play food (include food from other cultures)

- ❏ plates

- ❏ cups

- ❏ utensils

- ❏ cooking supplies (measuring spoons, mixer, bowls, hot pads, wooden spoons, eggbeater, cookie cutters, aprons and smocks, rolling pin, muffin tin, whisk, colander, cutting board)

- ❏ variety of adult clothing (scarves, dresses, pants, jackets, suits)

- ❏ variety of adult shoes

- ❏ community helper uniforms

- ❏ wigs

- ❏ hats (including various occupational hats like firefighter, police officer, nurse, military helmet, etc.)

- ❏ baby dolls

- ❏ doll furniture (crib, high chair, stroller)

- ❏ mirror

- ❏ pictures of families

- ❏ a dresser

- ❏ coatrack

- ❏ telephone

- ❏ child-size table and chairs

- ❏ child-size sofa

- ❏ puppets

- ❏ puppet theatre

- ❏ ironing board and iron

- ❏ broom and dustpan

Block Center

Block Center is essential in developing problem-solving skills and classification. This area will also help develop different concepts such as math and language.

- Blocks help develop math concepts by giving the children opportunities for estimating, creating patterns, and counting.
- Having the children talk about and name structures they have created develops language.
- In working with blocks, children discover special relationships, achieve balance, and develop hand/eye coordination. This area requires a generous amount of space for large construction and expanded play.
- Putting this area next to the Dramatic Play Center will allow for open-ended play and the shared use of materials in both centers.

Types of Blocks

In this area you should have a variety of different shapes and kinds of wooden blocks, along with an assortment of accessories. There are many different types of blocks. Unit blocks, hollow blocks, and table blocks are the primary blocks that are available to young children.

> **Unit Blocks**
>
> Unit blocks are the traditional wooden blocks with rounded corners and edges. These are used to construct structures.

> **Hollow Blocks**
>
> Hollow blocks are large blocks built with an opening in the middle. These are light enough for a young child to easily lift and are used to make large structures they can put themselves into for imaginary play. For example, Mary and Mitchell are building a car. They choose to use the hollow blocks to make a bottom, seats, and sides to the car. Mary goes to Dramatic Play Center to get pillows to use on the seats and the picnic basket filled with food for the trip. Next, they climb in and sit in the car to reenact a recent car trip.

teacher tip

Block Center should be placed in an area in the room away from the quiet activities and busy traffic areas.

> **Table Blocks**
>
> Table blocks are small, often colored, and come in a variety of unusual shapes. These blocks are used for small construction and with small figures.

Labeling

Place the wooden hollow blocks and unit blocks on open shelves that have been labeled with a paper outline or silhouette for easy organization and cleanup.

Block Center (cont.)

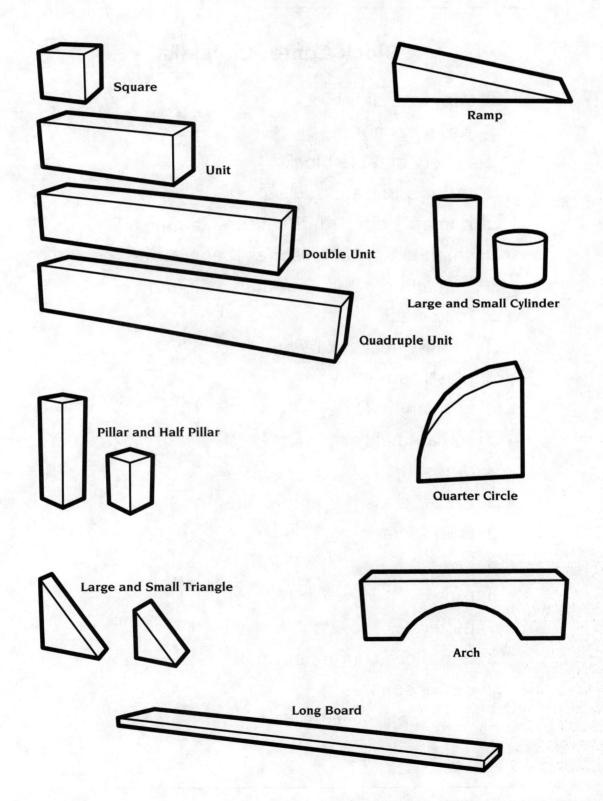

Square

Unit

Double Unit

Quadruple Unit

Pillar and Half Pillar

Large and Small Triangle

Ramp

Large and Small Cylinder

Quarter Circle

Arch

Long Board

Block Center (cont.)

Block Center Checklist

❏ variety of unit blocks

❏ variety of hollow blocks

❏ variety of table blocks

❏ trains and train tracks

❏ human figures (multicultural families)

❏ small people accessories (beds, tables, chairs)

❏ human figures (community helpers)

❏ road signs

❏ small-wheeled cars and trucks

❏ plastic structures

❏ farm animals

❏ zoo animals

❏ dinosaurs

❏ Easter grass (for animal life)

❏ fabric scraps

❏ boxes

❏ rope

❏ pulleys

❏ thin pieces of rubber tubing

❏ carpet squares

❏ large area rug with roads on it

Art Center

Art Center is a venue in which children can investigate and create, using a wide variety of materials. When the children are working in the Art Center, remember that it is the process the child is going through, and not the end product. Encourage and value originality rather than guiding the children to make their creations look like yours. Each child will create an original work of art while discovering the use of different materials to express an idea. One way of understanding a child's work of art is to listen to what the child is saying as he or she works with the materials. This is an educational opportunity introducing vocabulary words like *thick*, *mixture*, and the names of the materials the child has used. Ask questions and encourage them to talk as much as possible.

Displaying Art

When displaying the child's artwork, be respectful. Rotate art regularly and place it at the child's eye level. Try to incorporate art from each member in your class. This recognizes every child's effort. You can also display works of art from a well-known artist in Art Center. Doing so will not only create an aesthetically pleasing environment but will also develop an appreciation for the arts.

Location

This center should be placed in a well-lit area and close to a water source for easy cleanup. Use a plastic covering, such as a tablecloth on the floor or on the table, to prevent them from becoming covered in paint or glue. The art materials should be placed on low shelving and organized with pictures and labels. The Art Center should have a plentiful supply of materials that are age-appropriate, easily accessible, and of good quality.

Appropriate Praise

When a child approaches you with something he or she has just made, use appropriate praise. This will encourage more creative expression from the children in your class. Avoid using comments like, "I like your picture." When you put your validation on the children's art, they may start creating to please you. Use comments like, "You used red on this side and blue over here, but when mixed together you made purple." Make comments that reflect what has just been created. For example, "You made circles here using the yellow paint. How did you make the swirls inside?" Avoid saying "What is it?" since the child has worked hard on his or her creation and feels you should know what it is.

teacher tip

To create a frame for the children's art, simply place a colored piece of paper behind the picture a child has completed.

Art Center (cont.)

Appropriate questions to ask a child about his or her art:

* What is it made from?

* Tell me what is happening in your picture.

* Are you telling a story? What is it?

* What materials did you use?

* How were you feeling when you made this?

* What is you favorite part?

Documenting Language

- Once a child has had a chance to tell you about his or her creation, you can document the child's language either on the piece of art itself or on a separate sheet of paper.
- By documenting the child's language and labeling items in the picture, you are incorporating language and the written word into the art piece.
- Be respectful of the child if he or she says, "No, don't write on my picture." Do not write on the picture. The child might think you are destroying the art piece if you write on it. Always ask first.
- When documenting language, be accurate. Write it exactly as the child verbalizes it, even if it is improper language. This shows the child that his or her words have meaning.

teacher tip

When documenting the children's language directly on the creation, use a marker color that blends in with the picture. You don't want your writing to stand out more than the child's piece of art does.

Art Center (cont.)

Art Center Checklist

❏ glue and glue sticks

❏ blank paper in assorted colors

❏ variety of collage material (tinfoil, tissue, yarn, buttons, material scraps, macaroni, string, thread, lace, ribbon, felt, wood scraps)

❏ smocks, old shirts, aprons

❏ art easel

❏ paint

❏ variety of paintbrushes

❏ colored toothpicks

❏ construction paper

❏ scissors

❏ cornstarch

❏ crayons

❏ markers

❏ crepe paper

❏ drying rack

❏ finger paint

❏ finger-painting paper

❏ molding clay

❏ molding dough

❏ variety of cookie cutters

❏ stamps and stamp pad

❏ magazines, catalogs, greeting cards, newspapers

❏ paper punch

❏ pencils

❏ pipe cleaners

❏ stapler

❏ pottery clay

❏ tape

❏ foam trays

Art Center (cont.)

Recipes for Art Center

Uncooked Molding Dough

    1 cup cold water

    1 cup salt

    2 teaspoons vegetable oil

    Food coloring

    3 cups flour

    2 tablespoons cornstarch

Mix water, salt, oil, and enough food coloring to make a bright color. Gradually add in flour and cornstarch until the mixture reaches the consistency of bread dough. Store in an airtight container.

Cooked Molding Dough

    1 cup flour

    1 cup water

    1 tablespoon oil

    1 tablespoon alum

    1/2 cup salt

    Powdered drink for smell

    Food coloring

Mix all dry ingredients in a small pot. Mix in the oil, food coloring, and water in separate bowl. Slowly pour the liquid mixture into the flour mixture while stirring constantly. Cook over medium heat until the mixture has the texture of mashed potatoes and it pulls away from the sides of the pot. Remove from heat. Knead on work surface until smooth in texture. Store in airtight container.

Goop

    One part cornstarch

    One part water

    Tempera paint for color

Add the same amount of cornstarch and water in a bowl. Add tempera paint for color. Is the mixture a solid or liquid? Let the children explore. Throw in trash when finished.

Art Center (cont.)

Recipes for Art Center (cont.)

Peanut Butter Molding Dough (edible)

    1 cup honey

    1 cup peanut butter

    2 cups dry milk

Mix all ingredients together. Add more dry milk if the mixture is too sticky. Do not reuse.

Making Colored Noodles

    1 large recloseable bag

    1/4 cup vinegar

    Noodles of different shapes and sizes

    Food coloring

    Paper towels

Put the vinegar into the large bag. Next, put as many drops of food coloring as you wish in with the vinegar. The more food coloring you put in the bag the darker the color will be. Pour in the noodles. Fill the bag 3/4 full of noodles. Shake the bag, to color all the noodles. Finally, dump the noodles on the paper towels and allow them to dry. Use a variety of shapes and sizes for collage.

Great Bubble Mixture

    One clean large bucket

    10 cups cold water (distilled)

    1 cup dish soap

    3 to 4 tablespoons glycerin

Combine all ingredients and stir gently.

Science Center

The Science Center, sometimes called the Discovery Center, is an area in your class where the children will use and develop scientific understandings and experiment with concepts. Children are natural observers and have a sense of wonder. The Science Center is the perfect setting to meet the child's need for experimentation and invention. This area incorporates activities related to the scientific process of sorting, classifying, comparing, observing, and experimenting, and concepts such as shape, size, volume, and amounts.

Displaying Items

Items in the Science Center should be placed on a table or on a shelf in the quiet area of the class, close to a window.

- Include natural items such as plants, flowers, pinecones, seashells, and rocks.
- You may want to incorporate living creatures as well, such as fish, an ant farm, rabbits, guinea pigs, turtles, or other small animals.
- Rotating items in this center will also allow you to prevent the children from becoming bored.

Additional Themes

Incorporate themes such as the five senses, water, weather, seasons, plants and flowers, human anatomy, and objects that move. Children are curious, which makes them natural scientists. They are excited to discover as much about the world around them as they can. This area will help you make the most of the natural wonder children have.

teacher tip

By placing a bird feeder outside a classroom window, you are allowing the children to observe a wild living creature, bringing the outside in.

Science Center (cont.)

Science Center Checklist

- ❏ leaves
- ❏ mirrors
- ❏ microscope
- ❏ plants
- ❏ bug house
- ❏ flashlight
- ❏ kaleidoscope
- ❏ color paddles
- ❏ locks
- ❏ magnets
- ❏ magnet balls
- ❏ nuts and bolts
- ❏ simple machines
- ❏ magnifying glass

- ❏ telescope
- ❏ pendulums
- ❏ prisms
- ❏ rocks and seashells
- ❏ soil and a variety of seeds
- ❏ terrarium
- ❏ thermometers
- ❏ tuning forks
- ❏ watering can
- ❏ pictures of animals
- ❏ pictures of insects
- ❏ ruler
- ❏ scales

Sensory Center

Sensory, sometimes called the Sand and Water Center, provides opportunities for children to explore with different media and textures. In this center, children are using their small motor skills by scooping, squeezing, mixing, and measuring, along with developing critical thinking skills. Many sensory tables and bins are available commercially; however, a Sensory Center can easily be created with a large tub.

Safety

- Materials in this area need to be age-appropriate. If you are teaching toddlers, choose large objects that do not present a choking hazard.
- Water is a calming and relaxing material for the children and should be used often, but it does require you to change it daily.
- Remind the children not to put small objects in their noses or ears. If someone does get something stuck in the body, do not try to take it out, and do not have the child blow his or her nose. Often, the object gets pushed back in further. Immediately call the school nurse and the parents.
- Wipe out the inside of the bin with disinfectant when changing the contents. This will ensure that the center is clean and ready for the next sensory material. This area should be placed on a surface that is easy to sweep and clean, such as tile or linoleum.

Rules

Before allowing children to work in this center, a few rules should be established so the children are not getting the materials all over the classroom.

Sensory Center Rules
- What is in the sensory bin stays in the sensory bin.
- You must wear a smock.
- If something that belongs in the bin is on the floor, the children who are responsible for that item should clean it up.

Play with the Children

Being an active part of the children's sensory play gives you the opportunity to ask open-ended questions like, "Why do you think the sand is coming out so slowly?" or "What do you think would happen if you added water to that sand mound?" Asking open-ended questions allows the children to use and develop critical-thinking skills.

Sensory Center (cont.)

Sensory Center Checklist

- ❏ sensory bin
- ❏ lid to sensory bin
- ❏ smocks
- ❏ various-size molds
- ❏ sponges
- ❏ plastic bottles
- ❏ measuring cups
- ❏ measuring spoons
- ❏ small cars
- ❏ boats
- ❏ plastic piping
- ❏ eggbeaters
- ❏ funnels
- ❏ pictures
- ❏ turkey basters
- ❏ eyedroppers

- ❏ straws
- ❏ shovels
- ❏ buckets
- ❏ ladles
- ❏ sand combs
- ❏ noodles
- ❏ rice
- ❏ sand
- ❏ beans
- ❏ shelled corn
- ❏ cornmeal
- ❏ birdseed
- ❏ flour
- ❏ salt
- ❏ cotton balls

Music and Movement Center

Movement naturally occurs in young children. Children enjoy different beats, tempos, and tunes to which they can sing along, play, or move their bodies. The Music and Movement Center provides the children in your class with opportunities to develop coordination, express feelings, gain body awareness, gain confidence in the way their bodies move, and play musical instruments. Having this center as a choice at work time can be distracting, so have it located away from the quiet activities in the classroom.

Materials

In this area, the children should be provided with audio devices such as tapes and CDs, along with a wide variety of musical instruments on low shelving for easy access. There should also be a wide range of musical compositions from classical to today's top 40 available to the children to listen and sing to. The students will develop an appreciation for different types of music.

Rules

Establish some rules for the area, such as:

- Always be kind to any musical instruments.
- Keep the music at a respectable level.

Storage

The musical instruments should be labeled and the children should be expected to return them to their designated spots. Have scarves, ribbon sticks, beanbags, and other materials available for the children to use for creative expression. The area you have chosen for your Circle Time is an excellent spot for the music area to be. This area will have enough space for the children to move around freely.

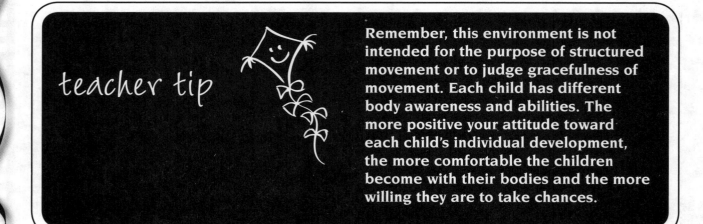

teacher tip

Remember, this environment is not intended for the purpose of structured movement or to judge gracefulness of movement. Each child has different body awareness and abilities. The more positive your attitude toward each child's individual development, the more comfortable the children become with their bodies and the more willing they are to take chances.

Music and Movement Center (cont.)

Music and Movement Center Checklist

- ❏ space for the children to move freely
- ❏ audio devices (CD or tape player)
- ❏ tapes
- ❏ CDs
- ❏ scarves
- ❏ ribbon sticks
- ❏ beanbags
- ❏ piano
- ❏ sheet music

- ❏ rhythm sticks
- ❏ guitar
- ❏ bells
- ❏ tambourines
- ❏ drums
- ❏ maracas
- ❏ triangle
- ❏ xylophone
- ❏ autoharp
- ❏ homemade musical instruments

Computer Center

Opinions on the use of computers in early childhood classrooms varies among adults. Some teachers or preschools feel that children spend enough time in front of computers and televisions at home, and preschool should be a place for hands-on activities. Others feel that computers are permanent fixtures in today's culture and provide children with educational opportunities with immediate positive feedback.

If the appropriate programs are available, this area can help the children develop their skills in:

- prereading
- language
- cause and effect
- problem solving
- hand/eye coordination
- classification
- small-motor development

Location

If you choose to have computers in your classroom, consider the following:

- Place computers away from direct sunlight, away from extreme hot and cold areas in the classroom, and away from the active areas of the classroom.
- Place computers on a table that is at the child's eye level and large enough for two children.
- Provide games that support critical thinking skills in math, language, science, and real-world applications rather than just games.

Working Together

- Allowing children to work in pairs allows for social interaction and cooperative problem solving. Children can talk about what is happening and what they should do next.
- Do not allow children to be in this area for more than 20 minutes.
- Set a kitchen timer, and when the timer dings it is time for those children to choose another area. This will prevent a child from sitting at the computer the entire hour of work time.

Rules

Before allowing children to work in this center, a few rules should be established so the children are not getting the materials all over the classroom.

Computer Center Rules

- The teacher is the only one who can change games.
- The equipment in this area is fragile and should be treated kindly.

Computer Center (cont.)

Incorporating the Computer into Other Areas

- The computer can also be incorporated with the writing area as a writing tool. Allow the children to use the word processing program to experiment with letters. Eventually, you will notice the children looking on the keyboard for specific letters and eventually typing environmental-print words and their names.

- The computer can also be used as a teacher tool. Allow the children to see you use the computer while modeling proper behavior. If the class is connected to the Internet, this allows the parents in the class opportunities to e-mail you or their child and allows the children to e-mail their parents. Both children and their parents enjoy getting messages.

Computer Center Checklist

- ❏ computers
- ❏ table and chairs
- ❏ age-appropriate educational games
- ❏ kitchen timer
- ❏ headphones

Writing Center

In the Writing Center, children are given opportunities to experiment with writing and the written word. By providing these opportunities, including reading daily to the children, you will notice an increase in the children's interest in these areas.

Range of Abilities

There will be a wide range of abilities in this center.

- You will have children in your class who may only be able to scribble and others who will be able to write several words or even sentences.
- Small-motor development and hand/eye coordination are both involved in the child's ability to write. Exposure to writing at this age is of utmost importance. The more a child is exposed to language, writing, and tools used in creating the written word, the more interested and able he or she will become.

Reading, Writing, Listening, and Speaking

Reading, writing, listening, and speaking go hand in hand.

- A child can't say a word that he or she has never heard.
- A child can't read a word that he or she has never said.
- A child can't write a word that he or she has never read.

Reading and writing are the foundations of success in school and throughout life. To create lifelong learners who enjoy and love reading, you need to instill within them the importance of language. The more you read to the children, have the children speak to you, and emphasize the importance of the written word, the more you are providing a foundation for the children in your class to be successful.

Documenting Language

When documenting the children's writing, use their exact words even if it is improper English. This gives value to their words, and they realize that their language has meaning and create a connection between print and speech.

Activities

Keep all activities in this area meaningful to the children. Encourage the children in this area to:

- make books
- write words they know
- copy environmental print
- experiment with letters

You may begin to notice some children in your class using inventive spelling. Encourage these children. Don't tell them they are wrong. Learning to read and write is a hard and difficult process every child will go through at his or her own pace. Your goal is to produce children who love reading and who become lifelong readers.

Writing Center (cont.)

Writing Center Checklist

❏ paper

❏ lined paper

❏ stapler

❏ staple remover

❏ hole punch

❏ scissors

❏ pens

❏ markers

❏ colored pencils

❏ pencils

❏ inkpad with alphabet stamps

❏ typewriter

❏ glue

❏ chalk and chalkboard

❏ dry-erase board

❏ word cards with sight words on them

❏ books with blank pages

❏ magazines

❏ pictures

❏ alphabet stencils

❏ picture dictionaries

❏ cards with the children's names on them

❏ sentence strips

❏ word/picture cards on a ring that relate to a theme (animals, food, flowers, community helpers)

❏ sequence cards

❏ ABC games

❏ alphabet blocks

❏ magnetic board with alphabet

Reading Center

Reading Center is a spot in the classroom where a child can sit and read independently. This area should be in a quiet, relaxing location next to Writing and Listening Centers.

Furniture

The Reading Center should be cozy and have pillows, blankets, a rocking chair, and child-size furniture where the children can relax. Some classrooms have plastic swimming pools or bathtubs filled with these soft materials on which the children can sit, relax, and read.

Reading Center Storage

You will also need some sort of book rack or shelving to store books on.

- Open-front bookshelves allow the children to see what books or reading materials are available, but you are limited as to the number of books you can put on them.
- Place only enough books on the stand to neatly fill it. If you put out too many books, the children will have a hard time putting them away, and books may be destroyed.
- Storing books in baskets sorted either by type of book (animal, people, nonfiction) or type of reading materials (magazine, newspaper, book) allows you to put out more reading materials, but may be confusing for the children when returning books.

Materials

Provide a wide variety of printed materials for the children. These materials can be picture books, children's books, nonfiction informative materials, books the children have written, magazines, or newspapers. Provide many different reading materials and a variety of print in this area for the children to read.

teacher tip

Limit the number of children allowed in this area to three to four. This will eliminate the area from becoming overcrowded and noisy.

Reading Center (cont.)

Reading Center Checklist

- ❏ soft, cozy materials (pillows, blankets, cushions)
- ❏ plastic wading pool or bathtub
- ❏ variety of books
- ❏ child-created books
- ❏ magazines
- ❏ newspapers
- ❏ book rack
- ❏ shelving with baskets or plastic buckets
- ❏ encyclopedias
- ❏ flannel board
- ❏ puppets
- ❏ toy slide show projectors with slides of stories
- ❏ finger puppets

Listening Center

The Listening Center is a center where the children can choose a book and listen to it being read aloud on either a CD or audiotape, either independently or with a friend.

Location

This center should be placed directly next to Book Center. The CD or tape player should be placed on a child-size table with enough room for two children.

Materials

Store the books together with the matching tapes in either hanging clear bags or clear reclosable bags.

- A hanging rack and hanging bags can be purchased at your local teacher supply store, or you can use clear bags kept neatly in plastic containers or baskets.
- Stories and tapes need to be kept in clear bags so the children can choose the story they want without digging through all the bags.
- When the children are done reading, the book and tape should be put together in the bag and put away before choosing another story. This will keep the books and tapes from getting mixed up.

Labeling Your Audio Player

On your CD player or tape player, place a:

- green sticker above the play button.
- yellow sticker above the rewind button.
- red sticker above the stop button.
- blue sticker above the eject button.

Explain to the class what each color and button represents. By doing so, the children can use this area without your help.

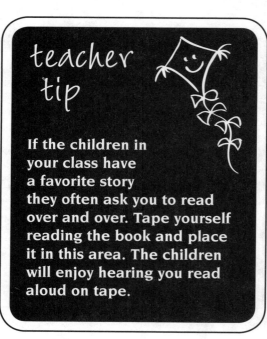

teacher tip

If the children in your class have a favorite story they often ask you to read over and over. Tape yourself reading the book and place it in this area. The children will enjoy hearing you read aloud on tape.

Listening Center (cont.)

Listening Center Checklist

- ❏ table

- ❏ chairs

- ❏ CD or tape player

- ❏ a variety of books with tapes

- ❏ clear bags for storage

- ❏ plastic bins, baskets, or hanging rack

- ❏ headphones

Maintaining Supplies

Resources can be categorized in two way: consumables and nonconsumables. All you need to be organized is a checklist of supplies that need to be reordered and how often. As a teacher, you probably have to turn in a list of necessary materials to the principal or director, and he or she will order materials in bulk for all the teachers.

Consumable Materials	Nonconsumable Materials
• Consumable materials such as markers, paper, crayons, clay, play dough, and paints need to be replaced often. • Consumable items can be ordered as often as quarterly or just two times a year, depending on how your school orders supplies.	• Nonconsumable materials are scissors, glue bottles, manipulatives, puzzles, shelving, art easel, resting mats and drying rack. • Nonconsumable supplies are usually ordered once a year. If your school only purchases large nonconsumable items once a year, keep a list of items that have broken or need to be replaced.

Maintaining and ordering classroom supplies is easy.

- Your school should keep a large supply of consumable materials, such as different types of paper, glue, paints, markers, crayons, and collage materials, on hand at all times.
- Some additional materials you will need are tissue paper, straws, shaving cream, squiggly eyes, and feathers.
- If your school doesn't have a form for you to keep track of the items you will need, go through your Month-by-Month Planning Sheet and try to predict what additional items you may need for the themes that are approaching.
- Request the items several months in advance.

teacher tip

See pages 81–82 for a list of holidays and common themes by month. This list can help you order supplies.

#50052—Managing an Effective Early Childhood Classroom   © *Shell Education*

Holiday and Theme Supply List by Month

Months	Theme	Butcher Paper for Bulletin Board	Miscellaneous Materials
September	• Getting to Know Me • I am a Can-Do Kid	• white • purple	• film to take pictures • butcher paper to trace the children's bodies • material scraps • squiggle eyes • yarn • wallpaper sample books
October	• Fall • Fire Prevention • Halloween • Safety • National Popcorn Week	• black • orange • red	• pumpkin • popcorn • orange glitter • yellow glitter • paper plates • tissue paper
November	• Native Americans • What I Am Thankful For • Manners • National Book Week	• brown • purple	• feathers • brown grocery bags • multicultural paper • multicultural markers • brads • plastic bookbinders
December	• Winter • Holidays Around the World	• blue • white	• any materials needed to make and wrap presents to parents • glitter • construction paper • plaster of paris • tissue paper • straw • pine tree • pipe cleaners • liquid starch • candles
January	• New Year • Animals That Live in the Snow • Hibernating Animals • Martin Luther King Jr. Day	• light blue • white	• New Year's Eve hats • noisemakers • fake snow • paper in multiracial skin colors • markers in multicultural skin colors
February	• Groundhog Day • Valentine's Day • Presidents' Day • Feelings	• pink • red	• envelopes • stickers • heart-shaped stencils • red glitter • paper doilies • red construction paper • white construction paper • pink construction paper

Holiday and Theme Supply List by Month (cont.)

Months	Theme	Butcher Paper for Bulletin Board	Miscellaneous Materials
March	• Dr. Seuss • Farm Animals • Zoo Animals • St. Patrick's Day	• green • blue	• red construction paper • white construction paper • cotton balls • yellow feathers • yarn • gold glitter
April	• Spring • Plants • Garden	• yellow • light blue	• variety of seeds • gardening tools • soil • containers for the children to plant seeds in • pastel-colored paper • green pipe cleaners
May	• Insects • Mother's Day	• light blue • orange	• Any materials you will need to make and wrap the children's Mother's Day presents • squiggly eyes • different-colored pipe cleaners • clear contact paper • clear plastic lids
June	• Transportation • Father's Day	• red • purple	• cardboard boxes for creating forms of transportation (You can ask parents for these in your monthly newsletter.) • paint • paper plates for steering wheels
July	• Summer • Independence Day • Ocean Animals	• blue • yellow	• red construction paper • white construction paper • blue construction paper • glitter • straws • star stickers • stars to glue on paper • ocean-animal rubber stamps • seashells • sand
August	• Camping • Getting Ready for a New School and Teacher	• brown • red	• tissue paper

Ordering Supplies

Ordering supplies is often done by the director or the school principal. Unless you are given a monthly allowance, you will not be responsible for ordering materials. If you are going to order materials, shop around. Some companies will be able to deliver the next day, while other companies take a month. Sometimes it is more cost-effective for you to go directly to the store and purchase the items. Prices will vary from store to store, along with the quality.

Quantities

When looking in a catalog or in the store, look for items that can be ordered and purchased in bulk or large quantities.

- Dozen: When you purchase by the dozen, you get 12.
- Roll: When you purchase by the roll, you get one roll of the item, such as ribbon or butcher paper.
- Set: When purchasing by the set, the catalog will state how many of each item you get for a specific price. For example, if you want to buy craft trays, you can get one set for $9.95. There are six items per set. Or, you can get a set of storage baskets for $4.94. There are 8 baskets per set. The amount of items will vary when purchasing sets.
- Unit: When purchasing by the unit, the catalog will state how many of the item you get for the price. For example, if you want to purchase large craft buttons, you may get one unit for $7.95, with 95 items per unit. Similarly, for $7.95 you will get one unit of small silver bells, with 200 items per unit. Again, the amount in each unit varies.
- Gross: A gross refers to 144 pieces. For example, if you purchase a gross of Halloween stickers for $1.99, you will receive 144 stickers.
- Bulk: You do not have to worry about craft items going bad, so buy items in bulk as much as possible. It will not only save you money, but the items left over can be stored and used at a later date. Items to buy in bulk include all craft materials, tempera paint, neon paint, glue, construction paper, finger painting paper, easel paper, shaving cream, and bulletin board paper.
- Paper: Construction paper can be ordered in two different sixes: 9 x12 inches (23 cm x 30 cm), or 12 x 18 inches (30 cm x 46 cm). It can be cost-effective to purchase the 12 x 18-inch sheets and cut them in half with a paper cutter when you need 9 x 12 inch sheets. It is also economical to buy large rolls of butcher paper for bulletin boards and not cover them with pieces of construction paper. Whatever you are ordering, compare prices at a number of stores. It may be cheaper for you to get paper from one store and to purchase paint at another.

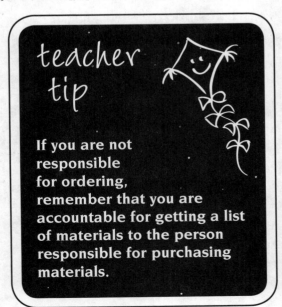

teacher tip

If you are not responsible for ordering, remember that you are accountable for getting a list of materials to the person responsible for purchasing materials.

Routine

A routine consists of regular and predictable activities that form your daily schedule. Having a routine in your class will help the children predict what comes next and establish a sense of passing time. Having an inconsistent schedule will cause stressful periods for the children and teachers. No one will know or be sure of what comes next.

- For example, if small-group time follows outside time, the children will be accustomed to getting into small groups when they return to class.
- Having a well-established routine will also make your job easier. You will not be telling the children constantly where to go or what to do.
- When a substitute comes in to a classroom that has a regular routine, you will hear the children say, "That's not what you do next" or "Next we go to our small groups." The children will be able to run the class by themselves.
- Planned transitions are also an important tool to your routine. Establish a song or finger play to be used at specific times of the day. For example, have the same song on a CD for cleanup time. Have the children's goal be to have the room clean by the time the song is finished. If you use the same song each time, the children will know just how long they have to get the room clean.
- When you want the children to have their eyes on you, use the same gesture or clap so they know exactly what is expected.
- If for any reason your schedule is going to change, let the children know as soon as possible. Some children thrive on the predictability of a routine and can become upset if not told about a change.
- Routines can also be established in group times as well. For example, when the children are doing the calendar activity, do the activity in the same order each time. When deciding on your classroom routine and schedule, keep in mind that children learn best when they have large blocks of time without interruptions.
- Just because you have a schedule doesn't mean it is set in stone. Be flexible and keep the children's needs and interests in mind. If all the children are actively involved in activities at work time but the clock says it is cleanup time, it won't be a problem if cleanup is put on hold for another 15 minutes. You may only have to adjust the schedule a bit and cut outside time by a few minutes. Sometimes, you may be involved with a group of children and lose track of time, which is perfectly okay. Just try to keep the schedule in the same order for those children who need the predictability of what comes next.

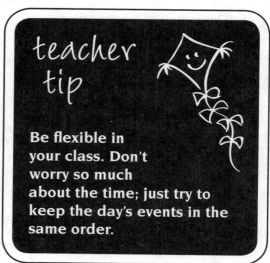

teacher tip

Be flexible in your class. Don't worry so much about the time; just try to keep the day's events in the same order.

Elements of the Day

Components of an early childhood program are:

- greeting the children
- teacher-directed activities
- circle time
- open work time
- outside time
- snack time
- transitions

These need to be included in your daily schedule. If you are in a full-day program, lunchtime and naptime will also be included in your routine.

Greeting the Children

When any child or parent walks into your class, you need to be at the door to greet him or her. It is common courtesy and good manners to say hello. Often this simple gesture is overlooked. Imagine how you would feel if you walked into a room full of your friends and no one said hello.

Daily Health Check

When you greet the child, you also have another motive. This is your chance to do a daily health check.

- A health check is when you are taking a quick look at each child, from head to toe. You are looking for any signs of illness.
- Start by saying "Hello, and how are you today?" You may even want to touch the child, checking the body temperature.
- Look at the child's face and look for signs of tiredness or any substance leaking from the eyes.
- This is also an opportunity for you to talk to the parents. If you notice that Johnny looks tired, you may want to ask, "Did Johnny sleep okay last night? He looks a bit tired." This opens the door of communication between you and the parents. The parent may tell you that Johnny was up last night with a nightmare, or tell you he was sick all night, in which case you need to follow your school's policy on sick children.
- Speaking to the parents each morning also lets the parents know you genuinely care for their children.

Greeting the Children

Parents Entering Your Class

Let the child show the parent something in the room or a project the child is working on. This is a wonderful opportunity for a parent to see the child in his or her daily environment, and will allow the child to share his or her accomplishments.

Dropping off the Child

- It is often difficult for a child to say good-bye to his or her parents. Give the parent a nod or a gesture to let them know it is time for the final good-bye. You then need to comfort the child in a gentle, nurturing way.
- Reassure the child that the parent will come back, and give the child a general time the parent will return. For example, you can say, "Your mommy will come pick you up after nap and snack time." This will give the child something to look forward to.
- When you have a child who is distressed often, remind the parents how important it is to be back at the school at the time they said they would return. When a parent tells the child he or she will be picked up right after nap and the parent doesn't show up until the end of the day, this may be causing some of the anxiety.
- Often the parent is upset watching his or her child cry as they walk away. The parent may feel guilty leaving a screaming child. Reassure these parents that their child will be fine, and if it would make them feel better to call later and see how their child is doing.
- You may want to have them leave a phone number to call if you are unable to comfort their child.
- Parents and adults are distressed by separation, too. Remember to be sensitive to both the parent and child.

Absent Children

- When a child is absent for more than three days and the parents have not phoned the school, make a phone call to see if the child or family is okay. Again, this will show you care about the family and the children in your class.
- When you are at circle time, point out who is missing. Let the children know the reason a child may be gone. If the child is sick, say, "Mattie has been sick for two days now and I am missing her," or "John is at Disneyland today. I know he is having a great time."
- Saying these nice things about a missing child will encourage the children to say nice things when the child returns.
- When a child returns, say positive comments like, "I am so glad you are back" or "Your friends really missed you. They are going to be so happy to see you." You will notice the children will approach the friend who has been gone and welcome him or her back.

Greeting the Children (cont.)

Opening Activities

Once you have greeted the child and he or she has entered the classroom, he or she needs to follow the same schedule each day. This will establish a morning routine.

- For example, have the children hang up their bags and coats, find their names, and put them into the Attendance Pocket Chart. Then, while waiting for the rest of the class to arrive, have each child find a book to read while sitting on his or her "sit-upon," which may be a piece of carpet, a hot pad, a fabric-covered magazine, or a similar item small enough for one child to sit on.
- There are other options in the morning routine if you don't want the children sitting at circle and reading. After the child finds his or her name, the child can choose from one of the centers you have selected to open.
- Do not open up more than three centers or you will have to have a cleanup time before morning circle.
- Open centers with specific choices such as moulding dough, bottle and cap matching, manipulatives, or paper and crayons. Keep the arrival activities simple and easy to clean.
- Once all the children are accounted for or you have waited five minutes into class time, call the children to morning circle time.

Attendance Chart

- As the children enter the classroom, have them find their names and place them in the attendance pocket chart.
- Have one row for all the girls and another row for boys to put their names.
- During opening circle, have a child count how many girls are present that day and how many boys.
- Discuss which has more and which has fewer.
- Have the child clip a clothespin with the corresponding number written on it on the row of girls' names and another on the row of boys' names.
- Then have the class count the total number of children present that day and state the correct number in the sentence.
- Use mathematical terms when doing the attendance chart. For example:
  - "Today we have five girls and six boys here."
  - "There is one more boy. So there are more boys here today."
  - "If we add up all the children, we have 11 friends here, so five plus six is 11."

Circle Time

Circle Time is a section in the day when all the children in your class will be sitting together. This is a structured time in the preschool day, but with less formal goals than a small-group time.

Circle time is for:

- reading stories and exposing the children to literature.
- doing music and movement activities.
- introducing the new theme and the calendar.

Allow the children enough time to finish cleaning, and encourage them to sing along or copy the pattern with you until everyone is sitting at Circle.

When you have the entire group of children sitting together, you will have some combinations of children who should not sit next to one another.

- To help solve this conflict and ensure personal space of each child, you can give the child one of the sit-upons, which will give the students a specific place to keep their bodies.
- Do not let the child move his or her sit-upon once you have placed it on the floor.
- By placing numbers or writing the children's names on the sit-upons, you have control of who gets to sit next to whom, and you will be able to keep children who cannot sit together away from one another.

Morning circle time is your opportunity to:

- assign jobs
- make announcements
- do the calendar
- report the weather
- have the children tell you about any "Happy News"

> **teacher tip**
>
> **Use a piece of carpet, a hot pad, or a fabric-covered magazine that has been labeled with the children's name as a sit-upon for the children to sit on at Circle.**

Length of Circle Time

Keep the Circle Time activities approximately 15 minutes long. Circle Time needs to relate to the core curriculum and be interactive. During Circle Time, someone should read aloud to the children.

Circle Time (cont.)

Show and Tell or Share Day

You can also incorporate Share Day or Show and Tell into one of your Circle Times. Once a week, on the same day each week, have the children bring something from home that is related to the week's theme. Encourage parents to send books and objects, but to avoid items that are violent, breakable, or so small that they may be lost.

Where to Put Share-Day Items

As the children arrive on Share Day, ask them to place their items into a basket labeled "Sharing." After all the children have arrived, put the basket on a counter out of the children's reach. They will be tempted to dig through the sharing box to see what is inside.

Let's Start Share Day

Before beginning the sharing Circle Time, designate a special chair or spot for the child to sit or stand to tell the rest of the class about what he or she has brought. Have the child begin by saying, "My name is _____ and I brought _____." Then, have the child tell the class about the item. Ask the child specific questions that require more than a yes or no answer.

Questions or Compliments

- After the child is done discussing the item he or she has shared, ask the class if they have questions or comments.
- Have the child who is sharing choose two friends who have their hands raised to ask a question or say something nice about what the child has just shared.
- Share Day is a great opportunity for children to have the full attention of the class and practice speaking to a large group.
- It also provides an opportunity for the other children to think of a question related to the object and to practice saying positive things to one another.

Assigning Jobs or Helping Hands

Assigning jobs to the children will encourage a community classroom atmosphere. Every person in the class has a daily responsibility. The jobs can be assigned daily or weekly. At the beginning of the year, or if you introduce a new job, explain what the child is to do and what your expectations are. When assigning jobs, use either a pocket chart or a bulletin board on which the job descriptions and representative picture are displayed.

teacher tip

Use cues such as singing a song, counting backward, or clapping your hands in a pattern to signal to the children that it is Circle Time.

Circle Time (cont.)

Examples of Daily Jobs and Helping Hands

- Calendar—Adds the numeral to the calendar and leads the class in counting the days that have so far passed in the month.

- Weather—Looks outside and draws or picks correct card to match the current weather.

- Line Leader—Leads the class when moving from the classroom to another part of the school.

- Counter—Counts the children on the Attendance Chart. Counts the boys and girls and places the appropriate numbers after the girls and boys. Then decides if there are more boys or girls at school. Finally, counts all the children.

- Chairs—This job is for two children. Have the children stack the chairs at the end of the day.

- Tables—This job is for two children. Have the children wipe off the tables after work time and after lunch and snack.

- Lights—Turns the lights off and on when asked to do so by the teacher.

- Sit-Upon Helper—Puts out the sit-upons and picks them up after circle.

- Book Collector—Collects the books from the children after quiet reading time.

- Pet Caretaker—Feeds and changes water for the classroom pets (if any).

- Messenger—Takes any messages to the office or other classrooms

If you are a full-day program, you may want to include the following jobs:

- Set table for lunch—This job should be for the same number of children as tables used at lunch. Have these children put the plates, cups, napkins, and utensils on the tables.

- Mat Helper—Helps put out the mats for rest time.

teacher tip

Use the "Helping Hand" pattern on page 91 to create a helpers bulletin board.

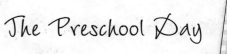

Circle Time (cont.)

Pattern for Helping Hands

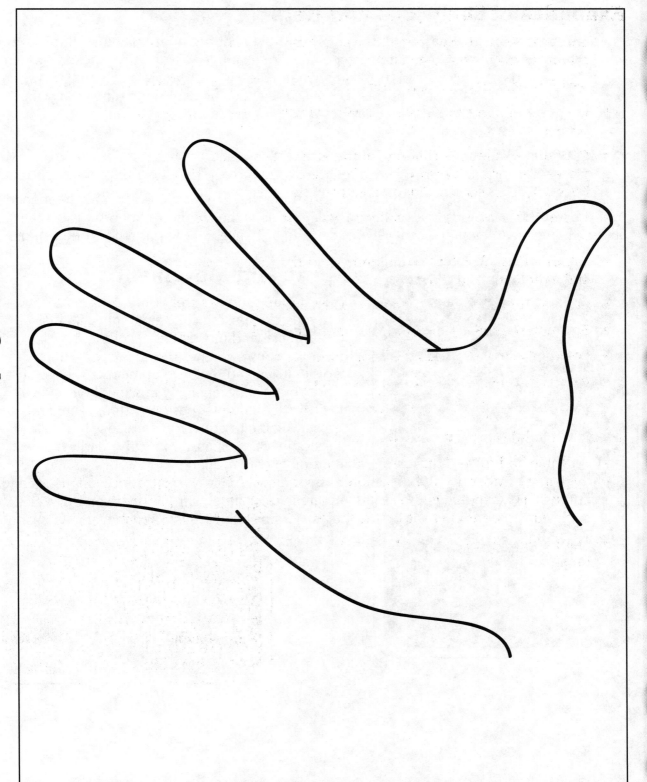

Circle Time (cont.)

Announcements

Announcement time is when you let the children know what activities will be available to them and let them know of any change in the schedule. For example, "Today is Wednesday, which means cooking day. Today we will be baking banana bread." Or, "We are also going to switch our outside time with Mrs. Smith's class because they need an extra-long time for a science experiment they are doing outside today."

Happy News

Mondays are the perfect day to do "Happy News" with the children. This is the children's opportunity to tell you anything. It can be something they ate for breakfast, what happened over the weekend, or a description of a play date. This is the children's opportunity to talk about what is meaningful to them. Give each child a chance to talk while the group listens.

teacher tip

When having the entire class do any activity, especially with music, musical instruments, and movement, you need to model the expected behavior. If you want the children to crawl on the floor like bugs, you need to be on the floor crawling like a bug with the class. Children learn through example.

Music and Movement

Large-group time is a great time to have fun with music. Exposing children to music, musical instruments, and movement encourages and develops body awareness, large motor skills, coordination, and the development of the whole child. Young children enjoy moving their bodies to music with different types of rhythms. There are many tools available to educators for use with music in the classroom. CDs, tapes, and child-friendly musical instruments are available at any educational store. Music is also a fun way to introduce languages and unfamiliar instruments from other countries. See page 93 for a sample music and movement lesson.

Circle Time (cont.)

Music and Movement Lesson—Sample

Concept: Language Development, Following Multiple Directions   **Time:** 10 minutes

Materials Needed:

1. A record or CD player. A CD or tape with rhythm stick activities on it.
2. Rhythm sticks

Vocabulary: *smooth, bumpy, tempo, rhythm*

Procedure:

1. Give each child two rhythm sticks, one smooth and the other bumpy. Have the children put their sticks down on the floor in front of them in a teepee formation. Refer to this position as the "Quiet position."
2. Have the children pick up the bumpy stick. Then have them pick up the smooth stick and have them rub the smooth stick over the bumpy stick. Ask them, "What does it feel like?" and "What does it sound like?" Have the children return the rhythm sticks to the "Quiet position."
3. Reverse the directions. Have the children pick up the smooth stick first, then pick up the bumpy stick. Have them rub the bumpy stick over the smooth one. Ask the children, "What does it feel like?" and "What does it sound like?"
4. Turn on the rhythm stick record or CD and have the children follow the directions. The group will have a hard time at first changing tempos and rhythms with the music but the more the children are exposed the easier it will be come.

Alternate Activity: Rhythm sticks can also be used as a "following direction" or "copy me" activity. Have the children keep their sticks in the "quiet position" and have them watch you as you start out with a one or two step sequence. For example, hit the sticks on the floor and then above your head. You put your rhythm sticks in the quiet position and have the children repeat what they have just observed. Add another element to your sequence when the children are able to easily follow your example.

McREL Music Standard 2: *Performs on instruments, alone and with others, a varied repertoire of music.* Skill:1.

McREL Music Standard 6: *Knows and applies appropriate criteria to music and music performances.* Skill:1.

Circle Time (cont.)

Calendar Activity

The calendar is an important tool for the early childhood classroom. It allows the children to:

- visualize what is coming in the future.
- remember what has happened in the past.
- have daily practice with vocabulary words.

You can mark special days such as birthdays on the calendar by placing a picture of a child on the date of his or her birthday, or a picture of a cake. The students will begin to count the squares on the calendar and tell their friend how many days until his or her birthday. Mark any special vacation days that may be coming up. See page 95 for a sample calendar lesson.

Remember to include special multicultural dates, such as Hanukkah, Chinese New Year, and Kwanzaa. You can also mark on the calendar any dates on which you know you might be absent. This also allows the students and parents to prepare for a substitute. The calendar activity is also a job you have assigned to a child in your class. Allow this child to place the number representing the special day on the calendar and count up to that day from the present day.

Weather

Recording daily weather is a great way to introduce graphs and change in the environment. On a large piece of paper, draw a monthly calendar. Mark any days the school is closed. This chart will look like an empty calendar. Next to the weather calendar, have the weather choice cards available.

Remember to keep it simple. You can always use the pattern included in this book. Have the weather person go to the window and describe what it looks like outside. Next, have the child come back to the chart and in the proper square on the empty calendar have the child draw the weather. At the end of the month, count how many days were sunny, rainy, cloudy, stormy, and snowy in the month, and make the monthly weather graph.

teacher tip

Have the children practice using different voices (talking, whispering, shouting, and singing) during Circle Time and discuss what type of voice should be used at work time.

Circle Time (cont.)

Calendar Lesson—Sample

Concept: Language Development

Materials Needed:

1. The days of the week are written in one color.

2. The months of the year are written in another color.

3. The words "Today is" are written in black.

4. Numbers one through nine are written in the fourth color. Make sure you have two number ones and two twos. These will be needed for eleven and twenty-two.

Having each part of the sentence either on a different color paper or written in a different color marker will help the children identify the parts of the sentence. "Today is" is written in black and will stay on the bulletin board. This will help these words become part of their sight word vocabulary, words the children will not have to sound out as they will become automatic.

Time: 10 minutes

Procedure:

1. "Today is _____, _____ _ _." The students need to correct this sentence.

   "First we need to figure out what day of the week it is today. Yesterday was Tuesday."

2. Take out the days of the week cards. Do not go through the days of the week in order. Mix them up so the children have to think about the word "yesterday." Use the cards like flash cards. Holding up the Monday card say, "Is today Monday?" The children will respond, "No." While holding up the word "Wednesday" ask, "Is today Wednesday?" The children respond, "Yes." Place the day of the week card in the correct spot in the sentence on the bulletin board.

3. Next in the sentence is the month of the year. Do not take this down each day. On the first day of the month go through the month cards. Place the month in the proper spot in the sentence.

4. Finally is the date. Have a calendar on the bulletin board below where the "Today is" sentence.

   - If you have a reusable calendar put the date on the calendar each day or have an already printed calendar and cross off the days of the week as you go along. Either way works well.

   - Point to the correct date on the calendar and ask the children if the date on the calendar matches the one in the "Today is" sentence. The students should respond "No." The sentence should have yesterday's day and date up until the class decides how to change it to make it correct each day.

   - Ask the students which number doesn't match. If yesterday's date was the 24th , point to the two and ask, "Does this number match the first number on today's date on the calendar?" The students reply, "Yes."

   - Next ask, "Does the four match the number on the calendar?" Students reply, "No."

Circle Time (cont.)

Calendar Weather Cards

Circle Time (cont.)

Calendar Weather Cards

The Preschool Day

Read-Aloud Time

Read-aloud time is when the entire class is together for a shared reading experience. The event of reading a book to a class is not just you reading and the group listening. This should be an interactive time for the children's input, thoughts, and feelings. Make sure that every child can see the book. Have the children sit on their sit-upons in a semicircle or in rows. When reading to children, remember to hold the book facing the children about shoulder height and slowly move the book around the circle. See page 99 for a sample read-aloud lesson.

- Begin by showing the children the cover of the chosen book and ask the class what they think the story may be about. Remember, there is no wrong answer. Ask open-ended questions like, "Why do you think that?" or "What gave you that idea?" Encourage conversation.
- Next, open the page and tell the children who the author is, and explain that an author is the person who wrote the words in the book and that he or she is the one telling the story.
- Next, tell them who the illustrator is and explain this is the person who drew the pictures. Then begin reading the story. Encourage the children to ask questions about the story. If they don't know what a word means and never get the opportunity to ask, an educational moment is lost.

Extensions of Reading Aloud

Reading aloud to your class is important, but giving the children opportunities to extend the reading experience is also important. You can stop in the middle of the book, put it away, and tell the class that they get to write the ending to the story. Then the shared reading becomes a writing and illustrating moment. The class can create a new ending together or individually. To have the class decide and create an ending together, you will need to document the children's language on a language experience chart as they give new endings to the story. Small-group time is a good time to document the children's language. This way, you can focus on the ideas of a few of the children and help them expand their thoughts. The children can also independently write and illustrate an ending. By allowing the children to become illustrators and draw pictures that correspond with their new ending, you are giving each child an opportunity to be creative and use his or her own ideas.

Flannel Board

Read-aloud time is also a time where flannel-board stories, retelling a story, and finger plays can be done for the children. Flannel-board stories are enjoyable for children of this age. Once read-aloud time is over and work time begins, leave the flannel board out as a choice at work time. The children will retell the story and may change parts to create an entirely new fable.

Read-Aloud Time (cont.)

Drama Activity

Put a twist on read-aloud time and turn it into a drama activity. After reading a story the children have shown great interest in, have the class act it out.

- Assign characters to several of the children in class.
- Explain that some of the other students need to be the audience, and explain that an audience is an important element in a play.
- The audience claps, smiles, and listens to the story.
- You will have to reenact the story several times to allow everyone in the class to be a character. If a child doesn't want to be in the play, do not force him or her. Be respectful of his or her feelings.

Read-Aloud Lesson for Large Group Time—Sample

Story Time/Concept: Language Development and Prediction

Time: 15–20 minutes

Vocabulary: *author, illustrator*

Materials Needed:

The book *Chrysanthemum* by Kevin Henkes

Procedure:

1. Show the class the cover of the book and ask for predictions about the story.
2. Open to the first page and read the author and illustrator name, explaining what each one contributed to the book. An author writes the words and an illustrator draws the pictures.
3. Begin reading the story and stop in random spots to ask the children what they think may happen next.
4. Once you have finished reading the book, turn to the beginning and tell the children they are now going to tell you the story.
5. As you turn the pages ask the children what happened on each page.

Expanding the story: At small-group time have the children complete the sentence, "I like my name because_____." and have them draw a picture of themselves. For an art activity, have each child's name written on a piece of paper and have the child decorate his or her name with a variety of collage materials.

McREL Language Arts Standard 5: *Uses the general skills and strategies of the reading process. Skills:* 1, 2, 3, 4, 5, 10, 12, 13.

McREL Language Arts Standard 6: *Uses reading skills and strategies to understand and interpret a variety of literary texts. Skills:* 1, 2, 4, 5.

McREL Language Arts Standard 8: *Uses listening and speaking strategies for different purposes. Skills:* 7, 8, 11.

Teacher-Directed Small-Group Activities

Teacher-directed activities are essential to a preschool class.

- Teacher-directed activities provide structure and allow for exposure to new topics for young children who will soon be entering the school system.
- A teacher-directed activity is any activity in which the teacher controls what will happen next.
- These activities have an objective or goal, a specific order which things are done, and a result.

Working with Small Groups

Small-group times are perfect for teacher-directed activities with six or fewer children. Some examples of teacher-directed activities are:

- performing science experiments
- asking the children questions and giving instructions to lead them in a specific direction
- working on a task the children are having trouble with, such as recognizing letters, counting, cooking projects, or brainstorming what they already know when you are introducing a new topic

Teacher-directed activities prepare the children for the more structured environment of the school system, yet in the preschool class it is a small amount of time a child is required to be in the formal learning environment each day. See page 101 for a sample teacher-directed small group lesson.

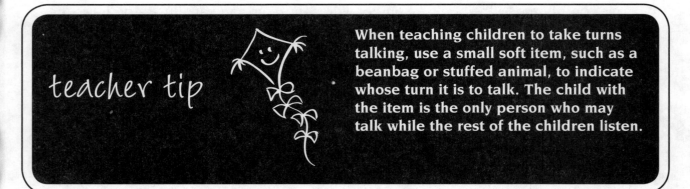

teacher tip

When teaching children to take turns talking, use a small soft item, such as a beanbag or stuffed animal, to indicate whose turn it is to talk. The child with the item is the only person who may talk while the rest of the children listen.

Teacher–Directed Small Group Activities (cont.)

Teacher-Directed Small Group Lesson—Sample

Describe an Apple

Concept: Language Development: Using Descriptive words

Time: 20–30 minutes

Materials Needed:

1. Red, yellow, and green apples
2. Large piece of paper (language experience chart)
3. A marker

Vocabulary: *crunchy, hard, soft, bitter, sour, sweet, mushy*

Procedure:

1. Hold up an apple and have the children tell you what it is.
2. Have the students tell you as much about the apple as possible by just looking at it.
3. Document the children's language as they describe the apple.
4. Cut up the red apple giving each child a piece. Tell them they cannot eat it until everyone has a piece.
5. As a class, taste the apple at the same time. While the children are eating ask them not to talk.
6. Ask them the following questions and remind them not to answer yet but to think of the answers in their head.
    - Is the apple sweet or sour?
    - Is the apple crunchy or soft?
    - What does the apple smell like?
    - What does the apple remind you of?
    - What things can you do with an apple that tastes like this?
7. Repeat the steps above with yellow and green apples.

Conclusion: When the children are done tasting all three types of apples you will review as a group what the children experienced. On one piece of paper have the word "red apple" on the top with a picture. Under "red apple" write the student's language describing a red apple. Encourage descriptive language. Document the students' language for the other kinds of apples as well. At the end of the activity the list made after tasting, touching, and smelling the apples will be much longer and more descriptive than the list made by just looking at the apple.

McREL Language Arts Standard 8: *Uses listening and speaking strategies for different purposes. Skills:* 1, 2, 4, 7, 8, 14.

Work Time

Work time is when a child gets to decide in what center he or she wants to play or work. This is the most important time in the day and needs to be valued. Children learn best through play that is active, with hands-on activities. This section of the day provides time and space for each child to be in charge of the situation. The child is free to pretend, problem-solve, develop language, relate experiences to the present situation, and work on social-emotional development. As the teacher, you need to plan for children's play by providing an environment that is constructive to play.

- Play helps develop cognitive development by allowing children to test ideas and practice social role behaviors they have observed.

- Language and social development during play depends on the child's ability to interact with his or her friends. The more they do it, the better they become.

- Practicing verbally and nonverbally through problem solving and negotiating with peers allows for a child to respond to feelings that a friend may be experiencing. As the children work through conflicts, they build the ability to understand conflict resolution. A parent or teacher will not always be available to solve a conflict. The children need to learn how to solve conflicts and work problems out themselves.

- As a teacher, you need to provide situations for problem solving and socialization with peers. These are important tools for a child to learn and will help the child through his or her entire life.

- Expressing feelings is essential to emotional development.

- Re-creating events in a safe environment allows children to work through feelings and experiences.

- You may find a child reacting to an event in his or her life that was emotionally difficult, such as remembering the death of a pet, being afraid of the dark, overhearing arguments by parents, or recalling something he or she saw on television.

- These experiences may be acted out in Pretend Center or Block Center, or illustrated in Art Center. Remember, it is healthy for a child to try to figure out his or her environment and where he or she fits in. Reenacting situations is a way of doing so.

In a full-day program, work time should be about one hour long. When children have long blocks of time, their play is more constructive, cooperative, and more meaningful than in short interrupted time periods.

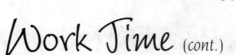

Work Time (cont.)

Planning Board

A planning board, also known as a Choice Board, can be constructed of pegboards, low bulletin boards, foam boards, or any other flat sturdy material that can be placed at the child's eye level.

- The planning board should have a designated area for each center and include a specific number of hooks or spots for the children to put their names on the choice of where they will work at during work time.
- A planning board allows the children to look at all the choices in the room and make a decision of what center to work.
- Allow time for planning in your schedule. This is usually done at the end of circle or just after returning from outside, and just before work time or free play.
- When planning, ask the children what area they are going to work and what they are going to do there. Allow enough time for the children to make a decision and tell you about it.
- Using a planning board also allows you to limit the amount of children in an area or completing an activity. This will also eliminate a child having to wait long periods of time for his or her turn. For example, seven children in Block Center who are all trying to build won't have enough space. The Block Center may only have four arch-shaped blocks, so a child needing the arch-shaped block may have to wait or never get to use the block if other children are using it.
- After deciding what area each child would like to work in, the children put their names next to that particular area that is labeled with the word and picture.
- This encourages independence and decision making, and develops planning skills.
- When a child is finished in an area before work time is over, that child must return to the planning board to move his or her name to a new area. When doing so, the child will look at which areas are full and which areas have spots available, again developing decision-making and problem-solving skills.
- If you want to take your planning board a bit further, you can put numbers on the board under the spots available in each area. This will help develop one-to-one correspondence.

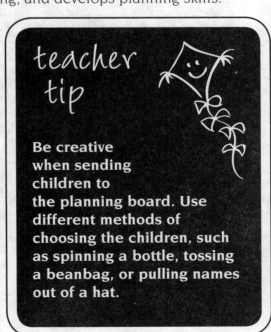

teacher tip

Be creative when sending children to the planning board. Use different methods of choosing the children, such as spinning a bottle, tossing a beanbag, or pulling names out of a hat.

Work Time (cont.)

Planning Board—Velcro Method

Materials Needed:

- bulletin board or foam core board
- pieces of Velcro (enough for each child's name and the spots in each center)
- rubber cement
- bulletin board boarder
- black marker
- pictures of children working in each center (See a pages 107–112 for Center Signs, or take real photos.)
- labels for each area (either typed or handwritten)
- the children's names (either typed or handwritten) glued on card stock and laminated. If you make the children's names large, you will need a large planning board.

How to Make:

1. Take either a bulletin board or a foam core board that you can either nail or stick to the wall and place it close to the ground so it is easy for the children to reach.

2. Rubber cement the pictures of each center, leaving enough room between for the Velcro spots.

3. You can either label the areas across the top horizontally (placing the tabs for the children's names directly under the picture), or you can label the areas going vertically (placing the number of spots going left to right after the label).

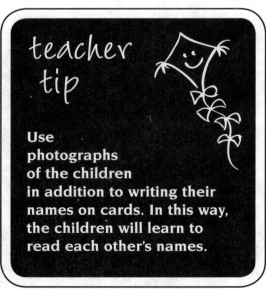

teacher tip

Use photographs of the children in addition to writing their names on cards. In this way, the children will learn to read each other's names.

4. Decide how many children you want working in each area and stick scratchy part of the Velcro on the board. For example, if you want only four children at a time in the Art Center, only put four Velcro spots on the board next to the Art Center.

5. Number the spots, using a black marker either above or to the left, depending on how you laid out your planning board.

6. Surround the bulletin board with a bulletin border.

7. Attach the soft side of the Velcro to the back of the children's name cards.

Work Time (cont.)

Planning Board—Clothespin Method

Materials Needed:

- construction paper
- pictures of children working in each center (See a pages 107–112 for Center Signs or take real photos.)
- black marker
- circle stickers
- stapler
- rubber cement
- clothespins
- bulletin board

How to Make:

1. Place the piece of construction paper vertically in front of you.
2. Fold the bottom of the paper up about one third of the way, creating a pocket.
3. On the front of the pocket, glue the name of the center.
4. On the top part of the construction paper, rubber-cement a picture of the children playing in the area. You can either use the following pictures or take photos of the children in your class.
5. Unfold and laminate the pockets.
6. After the paper has been laminated, refold the paper to re-create the pocket and staple the pocket along the side of the paper.
7. Decide how many children you want working in each area and place that number of circle stickers on the front of the pocket above the center name.
8. Number the circle stickers with the black marker.
9. Staple each area's pocket chart to a bulletin board that is easy for the children to reach.
10. Write each child's name on a clothespin.
11. The children simply move their clothespins when changing areas.

Work Time (cont.)

Planning Board— Pegboard Method

Materials Needed:

- a large pegboard
- spray paint
- hooks (enough for the number of children you want in each area)
- photocopies of the "Center Signs" (pages 107–112), or take photographs of the children working in each center
- metal tops to frozen juice cans (one for each child in your class) with a hole drilled in each top
- pictures of each child
- contact paper

How to Make:

1. Spray-paint the pegboard a bright color and let dry overnight.
2. Use contact paper to place the pictures of children working in each area to the pegboard. Make two rows, either horizontal or vertical.
3. Decide how many children you want working in each area and place that number of hooks next to the picture.
4. With permanent marker, write the child's name on one side of the frozen juice lid and use contact paper to place the child's picture on the other side. This method works well with children who are in the process of recognizing their names.

Center Signs

Block Center

Dramatic Play Center

Center Signs (cont.)

Task Center

Art Center

Center Signs (cont.)

Science Center

Sensory Center

Center Signs (cont.)

Music and Movement Center

Computer Center

Center Signs (cont.)

Writing Center

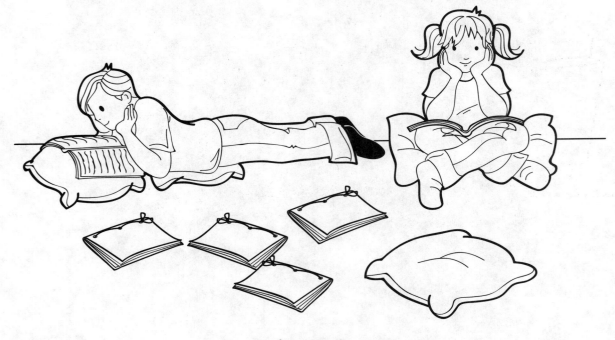

Reading Center

Center Signs (cont.)

Listening Center

Outside Time

Outside time is when the children are actively involved in outdoor activities. The outside area should have several large-motor activities. Providing a variety of large-motor choices and experiences are essential in the development of large-motor skills and coordination. Problems happen when the children are bored. If you begin to notice fighting or children just wandering around, bring something new to the outside environment. If you are in a full-day program, you should allow for one hour of outside time twice a day. Children today are spending less time outdoors. Some would rather be inside playing computer games and watching television. Encourage large-motor play outside as much as possible as encouragement to healthy lifestyles.

Noncompetitive Games

Noncompetitive games do not include a winner or first place. An example of a noncompetitive game is the parachute. The parachute can be used with balloons, balls, or alone, but the group of children should be working and playing together. There is no winner or first place in parachute play. You can play musical chairs; just don't take a chair away. The children enjoy dancing around the circle and looking for the empty chair.

Sand and Water

Water and sand tables need to be available for outside play. Occasionally, provide different media. The outside area needs a sandbox or sand area with water relatively close for digging and experimentation; this is essential in an outside atmosphere.

Bringing the Inside Out

Your outside environment should have some of the same elements as does your classroom.

- **Quiet Space**
  Lay a large sheet on the ground and place books and puzzles on it to provide a quiet area for children who need a quiet space.

- **Blocks**
  Take the hollow blocks outside to give the children a larger space to in which to build.

- **Art**
  Supply art material such as markers, colored pencils, a stapler, stencils, and tape to give the children another choice at outside time. Another way to incorporate art outside is to provide large pieces of paper and allow the children to paint with large objects such as feather dusters, brooms, and paint rollers.

- **Music**
  Occasionally provide music and tools to dance with, such as scarves and ribbon sticks for music and movement. You can also bring out baby dolls, hats, or play food with dishes to bring dramatic play outside.

Outside Time *(cont.)*

Outside Area Checklist

- ❏ bikes
- ❏ scooters
- ❏ wagon
- ❏ swings
- ❏ balance beam
- ❏ climbing structures
- ❏ balls of all sizes
- ❏ large plastic animals
- ❏ small plastic animals
- ❏ area for running and structured, noncompetitive games
- ❏ sensory table
- ❏ sand
- ❏ a variety of sand toys (buckets, shovels, scoops, funnels, molds, rakes)
- ❏ large plastic cars and dump trucks

- ❏ child-size brooms
- ❏ hula hoops
- ❏ basketball hoops
- ❏ play tunnels
- ❏ beanbag toss games
- ❏ jump ropes
- ❏ low-to-the-ground plastic slide
- ❏ parachute
- ❏ hopping sacks
- ❏ hop-along balls
- ❏ bubble tub and a variety of bubble wands
- ❏ bowling game
- ❏ ribbon sticks
- ❏ scarves

Snack Time

Snack time is when the children are given something small to eat during the day. This allows the children to refuel, relax, and take a break. Snack time can be a part of your schedule or can be considered as Open Snack. Open Snack is when the children can eat when they become hungry during work time. This area should be treated as a work area or choice at work time. Provide a space on the planning board for the children to select a snack area as a choice. The snack should include two food groups. The school usually provides snacks, but parents will often want to bring something for a birthday or a special holiday. (Be sure to check your school's policy on parents providing snacks for the class.)

Open Snack

If you choose to have snack time as part of work time, you will need to start out by setting limits on how much food a child can eat.

- Make four-by-five-inch food cards by placing a picture of the food item and the amount the child may take on each card.
- For example, if you are going to have cheese and crackers, on one card place a picture of crackers with the number the child may take. On the second card, place a picture of cheese with the number of slices the child may take.
- Having Open Snack also allows the children to practice self-help skills and responsibility.
- Each child will need to serve himself or herself and clean up the table when done.
- For the first few weeks, you will need to monitor the Open Snack area, or one child might eat all of the food intended for the entire class.
- If the snack requires the child to take one scoop of something, put out that particular size of scoop as an example. For example, one scoop of raisins is going to be smaller than one scoop of fish crackers.

- You can also combine cards. If for snack time you are having veggies and dip, you can put out the celery and carrot cards together.

Having a cooking or food-preparation project as a small-group activity is an opportunity for children to cook items for the entire class to eat for snack time. Cooking or preparing food should be part of your weekly schedule, and you should try to make your snacks from scratch as much as possible. The educational opportunities in cooking are countless. The children will learn to measure, cut, chop, stir, blend, mix, follow a recipe, and so on. Preparing snacks for the class gives the children a sense of accomplishment. The "I Need Help" section of your monthly newsletter is the best place to ask parents for any special item or appliance you may need for a cooking project.

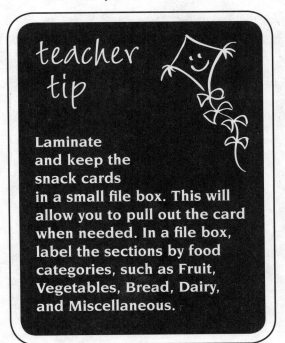

teacher tip

Laminate and keep the snack cards in a small file box. This will allow you to pull out the card when needed. In a file box, label the sections by food categories, such as Fruit, Vegetables, Bread, Dairy, and Miscellaneous.

Snack Cards — Fruit

Apple – 2 slices

Banana – half a banana

Orange – 2 slices

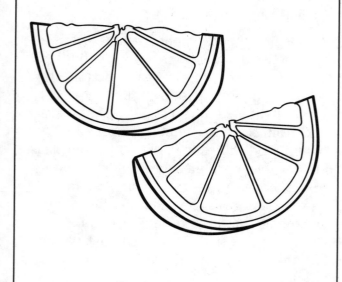

Raisins –1 scoop

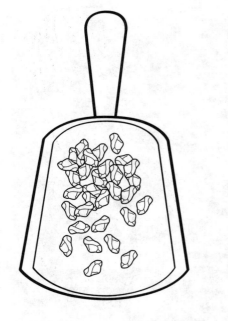

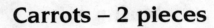

Snack Cards—Vegetable

Celery – 2 pieces	**Carrots – 2 pieces**

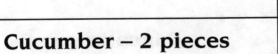

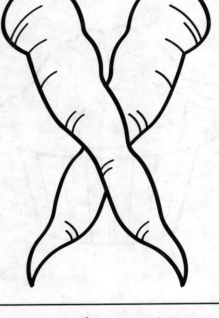

Cucumber – 2 pieces	**Broccoli – 2 pieces**

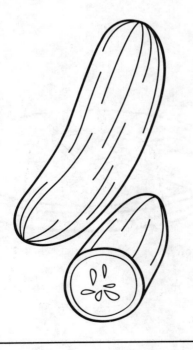

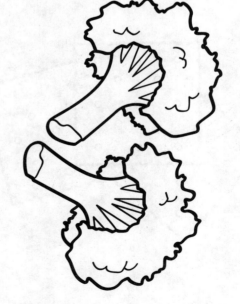

#50052—*Managing an Effective Early Childhood Classroom*

Snack Cards — Bread

Muffin – 1	**Bagel – Half**
	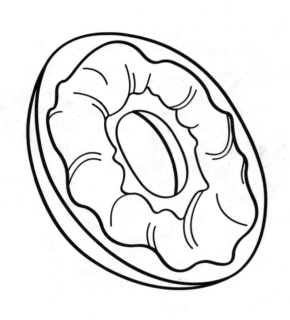
Saltine crackers – 3	**Pancake – 1**
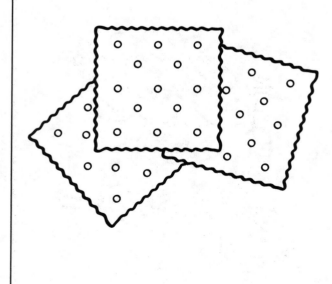	

Snack Cards — Dairy

Milk – 1 glass

Yogurt – 1 scoop

Yogurt

Cheese – 2 slices

Pudding – 1 scoop

Snack Cards — Miscellaneous

Jelly – 1 spoonful 	**Cream Cheese – 1 spoonful** 
Syrup – 1 teaspoon 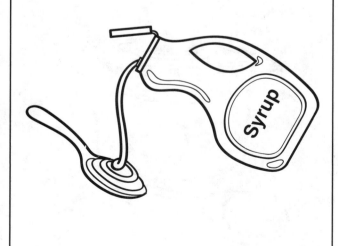	**Popcorn – 1 scoop** 

#50052—*Managing an Effective Early Childhood Classroom*

Cooking

Children today are growing up with fast food and full-time working parents. Opportunities for children to see their parents cook or helping their parents in the kitchen are diminishing. It is much quicker and easier for parents to go through a drive-through or pull dinner from the freezer than actually cook a meal. This is why cooking in the classroom is essential for creating healthy eating, as well as social and educational elements. When cooking with young children, be creative and allow the children to be completely hands-on. Have extra ingredients available just in case there is an accident. For example, if a recipe calls for two eggs, have four eggs available. Children have a hard time mastering the skill of cracking eggs, and having extra will allow the children to crack the eggs without you doing it for them. Start the year out with simple recipes that have the children practice and master simple skills before having the children cook difficult recipes, which require many ingredients.

Cooking with the Entire Class

When having the entire class cook or make snacks together, keep it simple with a limited amount of ingredients and with simple directions. Allow the children to have all the materials they need right in front of them and have them follow directions.

Ants on a Log

Give each child:

A piece of celery

A craft sick

Peanut butter

Five raisins

Dip each child's craft stick in the peanut butter then hand it to the child. Have the children spread the peanut butter inside the celery stalk and then place the raisins on top.

Ants on a log is an easy activity to do with the whole class. It only requires a few ingredients and one tool. The children will not have to wait for utensils or for another child to finish before they can participate. The entire class can do this at the same time.

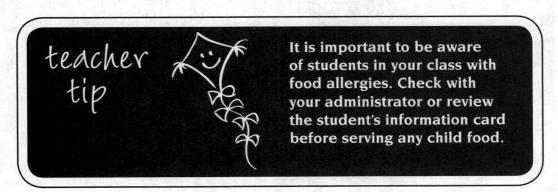

teacher tip

It is important to be aware of students in your class with food allergies. Check with your administrator or review the student's information card before serving any child food.

Cooking (cont.)

Cooking with small groups is fun and easy. Small-group time is when you have six or fewer children in a small, intimate setting.

- Cooking for the small-group activity will also allow the children to make enough food to serve the entire class because each small group will be making the same thing.

- Assign each child the responsibility of measuring and adding in ingredients when the recipe calls for it.

- Give each child the ingredient he or she is responsible for and a small cup or bowl to put it in when the child is done measuring it. This will allow the children to prepare their portions before they are needed.

- Giving the children small bowls or cups to put their ingredients in allows them to share measuring cups and spoons and allows you to watch and make sure the right amount is being measured.

- If you allow the children to hold their measuring utensils over the large bowl with other ingredients already in it, a child could spill or measure the wrong amount and ruin the entire cooking project.

- The recipe says to mix bananas and liquids first. First, Megan puts the bananas into the bowl. (Allow her to mash and stir.) Then she passes the bowl to Catarina, who adds in the milk, and so on.

- Allow each child to stir after he or she has added in the ingredient. The children are responsible for measuring and adding in the ingredients when the recipe asks for it.

teacher tip

Children recognize many product packages, product names, and logos. Use the packages you bring for cooking to draw students' attention to the print. See page 211-220 for more information on how to do this.

- Then all you need to do is read the recipe and be available when the children need help.

- You will repeat the same recipe with the next small group, making two of the same recipe to feed the entire class for snack.

- If the cooking experience is going to be the snack for the day, allow enough time for the food to cook and cool before serving. You may need to change your schedule to cook first thing in the morning to accommodate cooking times.

Cooking (cont.)

Small Group Cooking Lesson—Sample

Turkey Rice Treats: Thanksgiving and Turkey Theme

Time: 20 minutes

Makes: 12 turkeys

Materials Needed:

1. 6 cups chocolate rice cereal
2. 3 tablespoons butter
3. 1 package (10 oz.) marshmallows
4. Candy corns—one for each child
5. Red hot candy—two for each child
6. Pretzels
7. Vegetable spray
8. Peanut Butter

Procedure:

1. Melt the butter on low heat.
2. Remove from heat, add marshmallows, and stir until smooth.
3. Add in chocolate rice cereal and stir.
4. Let the mixture cool slightly.
5. Spray the children's hands with the vegetable spray.
6. Give each child a large spoon full of the rice cereal mixture to create a ball.
7. Give each child:
   - One candy corn (turkey's nose)
   - Two red hot candies (turkey's eyes)
   - 5 pretzels (turkey feathers)
8. 1 tablespoon peanut butter for the turkey's tummy (optional)

McREL Health Standard 6: *Understands essential concepts about nutrition and diet. Skill: 1.*

McREL Language Arts Standard 8: *Uses listening and speaking strategies for different purposes. Skills: 11, 13.*

McREL Visual Arts Standard 1: *Understands and applies media, techniques, and processes related to the visual arts. Skill: 2.*

Cooking (*cont.*)

When cooking with young children, you will need to have a variety of utensils and appliances.

Utensils	Appliances
• Measuring cups • Measuring spoons • Wooden and plastic spoons • Potato masher • Whisk • Mixing bowls • Knives (use only under direct supervision)	• Stove • Crock pot • Blender • Griddle • Hot plate • Toaster • Juicer • Hand mixer

Here are a variety of easy foods to make with your class. As you do more cooking projects with the class, you can add in some more difficult recipes.

Breakfast	Grains	Grilled
• Pancakes • Scrambled eggs • French Toast • Latkes • Applesauce • Crepes	• Breads • Muffins • Rolls • Rice • Cookies • Cakes • English Muffin Pizzas • Mac and Cheese	• Grilled Cheese • Grilled Peanut Butter and Jelly • Quesadillas
Blender • Smoothies • Malts • Peanut Butter	**Other** • Soups • Salads • Popcorn • Deviled Eggs • Lemonade • Orange Juice	

Transitions

Transitions are when a child moves from one activity to the next. In a classroom, transitions will consume a majority of classroom time if not planned out correctly. Using a planning board, a specific cleanup song, and a predictable schedule will stop the children from asking you what to do next.

Creative Transitions

When the entire group is required to change at one time—for example, going from Circle to Outside Time—do not just say "Line up," or you will have all the children making a mad dash to the door. Use different strategies in getting a few children to transition at one time.

Legs-out Method	Theme Information
• Have all the children put their legs out straight. Tell the children to look at their shoes. First, have all the children who have slip-on shoes line up. Then, the children who have buckles on their shoes can line up. Last, the children who have tie shoes can line up at the door.	• Ask the children to do something related to the theme before they can line up, such as naming a farm animal, a dinosaur, or a fruit or vegetable; or give an example of a tool a firefighter uses.
Pattern Method	**Pull Names from a Cup**
• You can also make patterns with the children as you call them to line up. Patterns may include boy/girl, long sleeve/short sleeve, long hair/short hair, or any other pattern you can create. The children enjoy trying to figure out what pattern you are creating and who will be next to line up.	• You can also use the tongue-depressor method. Write the children's names on tongue depressor sticks and store them in a cup or container where the sticks can stand upright. Begin by pulling out one stick. Read the name on the stick, and that child lines up. Repeat until the entire class is lined up. This is a random way of calling the children to transition. You may want to remind the children that if they are not sitting the right way, their names go back into the cup if they are pulled.

teacher tip

Keep transition times predictable, but be creative. Remember, some children do not like change and need a warning when a transition is about occur.

Cleanup

Cleanup time comes directly after work time. This is when the children are responsible for putting the used materials away. Cleanup time can be frustrating for both the children and teacher. First, create a routine. Having a specific song on a record or CD that the children are familiar with will help you from having to repeat "Cleanup Time!" For example, use the song "Zip-a-Dee-Doo-Dah" or "Mickey Mouse March." These songs are upbeat and long enough for cleanup, and the children know the words.

Five-Minute Warning

Give the class a five-minute, a three-minute, and a one-minute warning by showing them the number of minutes with your fingers while giving the verbal warning. This will help the auditory and visual learners in your class to know that cleanup time is coming. It will also eliminate a child being caught off guard and getting upset because he or she is not done yet. Furthermore, it gives the class some warning to start finishing up the projects they are working on.

As the Song Begins

- As soon as the children hear the beginning of the song, they will know it is time to stop what they are doing and start cleaning.
- At the beginning of the school year, establish some ground rules regarding cleanup.

Tell the class: "I do not pick up after you. You are responsible for putting away what you have worked with. Everything goes in a special spot, and they have been labeled for you. When you are done, find a friend who needs help."

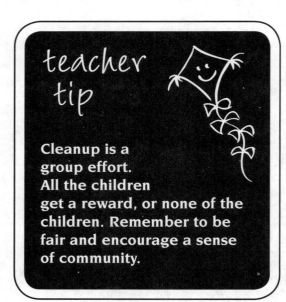

teacher tip

Cleanup is a group effort. All the children get a reward, or none of the children. Remember to be fair and encourage a sense of community.

Reward a Job Well-Done

The next step, if the group worked well together, is to reward a job well-done to establish a sense of community. See page 127 for two methods of rewards.

Cleanup (cont.)

Sticker or Rubber Stamp Method

- If the room is clean before the song is over, give everyone something special like smelly stickers or a rubber stamp on the hand.
- During the first few weeks, give them something every time they finish before the song is done.
- During the weeks that follow, gradually replace the concrete reward with thumbs up, or say, "Give yourself a pat on the back for a job well-done!"
- After a few months, the children will no longer require a reward. They will just be happy they got everything put away on time.
- Occasionally, give out the concrete rewards when cleanup was an outstanding group effort.
- If the class doesn't get everything put away on time, it is the group who doesn't get the reward. Do not single out one or two children; this will hurt their self-esteem. Just remind the class that, if they are done, to find a friend who may need help; and if they see someone not helping, remind them it is cleanup time.

The Marble Jar

Another option for reward at cleanup time is to use the marble jar. The concept of the marble jar is easy.

- At the beginning of the school year, bring out an empty plastic jar with a line drawn around the middle. Have a jar large enough to take the children some time to fill. Large peanut butter jars are good for this purpose.
- Each time the class finishes cleaning before the song is over, a specific number of marbles is placed in the jar.
- The goal is to fill the marble jar to the top.
- When the class fills the jar to the middle line, have the class take a vote on what kind of celebration they would like to have (ice cream party or popcorn and movie day).
- When the class successfully fills the jar to the top, invite parents to join the class for a grand party, such as a pizza party. Have the children create invitations, prepare the pizza, and plan the event.
- You can also use the marble jar in other ways. If you see the children performing random acts of kindness or if you see an outstanding job of teamwork, add a marble.
- Any time you emphasize positive behavior in a child, it can have a lasting effect. Once a marble has been placed in the jar, do not take it out. The class has worked hard to earn every marble placed in the jar.

Lunchtime

In a full-day program, lunch is usually served around noon. This is when all the children in the class sit at tables and eat lunch. Either a hot lunch made by the school cook or sack lunch brought from home is eaten at this time, depending on your program. Setting a routine for lunchtime will help this part of the day run smoothly. The children will know what to expect.

Prior to eating lunch, the children should wash their hands. Establish a procedure for using the sink in the classroom or for sending the children to the restroom so that nine students are not trying to use the sink at once. Consider playing music or doing finger plays with the children as they are individually or in small groups sent to wash their hands.

While Eating

- Create name cards to be placed on the table to identify where each child should sit for lunch. Fold index cards in half and write the children's names on the cards, one per card. Decorate with stickers and laminate for durability, if desired. The children must find their names in order to know where to sit each day. Mix up the seating arrangement each day. Assigning seating allows you to separate children, if needed.

teacher tip

By sitting at the table and eating with the children, you can model proper table etiquette.

- If the school provides the children's lunch, eating together family style is a special way to engage the children in conversation. Eating family style often requires the children to pass around the serving dishes and use their self-help skills. Preparing the table can be one of the jobs assigned to the children on the helper chart.
- The children will naturally carry on conversation during the course of lunch; however, be prepared to have a conversation starter to use if the conversation dies or becomes inappropriate. Conversation starters can be as simple as a question such as, "Would you rather go on a train or an airplane, and why?"

After Lunch

Routines for what happens after lunch may vary from school to school. The children have playtime outside at some schools. At other schools, the children go directly to nap time. Students should know what to do when they are finished eating. Either way, each student should be responsible for cleaning up the area in which he or she ate, as well as washing the hands and face.

Nap Time

Nap time is a quiet resting time for all the children. Young children need lots of rest. Tired children do not perform well in class. Nap time needs to have a routine, just like the rest of the day.

Establishing a Resting Spot

- First establish a spot where each child can place his or her mat.
- This designated spot is where the child will sleep every day. You may even want to draw a map of mat placement just in case you have a substitute.
- Assign spots to the children who don't sleep, or have a hard time falling asleep, that are apart from one another. This way there will not be the temptation to talk and play.

Allow Enough Personal Space and Encourage Self-Help Skills

- Try to allow space between mats; use the entire classroom.
- Encourage self-help skills by allowing the children to get all sleeping items needed and prepare his or her mat for rest.
- The children whose job it is to put all the mats on the floor should help you before lunchtime. This will allow the children to use the restroom and get on their mats right after lunch.

Setting the Mood

- Close the windows and doors, shut the blinds, and remind the children to rest their bodies.
- Walk around the classroom and cover any child who may need help with his or her blanket.
- Praise the children who are ready to rest.

Nap Time (cont.)

Reward for the First Sleepers

You can have a reward for the children who fall asleep first.

- Depending on the number of children you have resting, have between five to 10 small stuffed animals, such as small stuffed animals, in a bucket.
- About 30 minutes into rest time, quietly walk around the class and place a stuffed animal on the bottom corners of the mats of the children who are sleeping.
- Remember or write down the names of the children who fell asleep first.
- As the children wake up, they will look on their mats to see if they were one of the first to fall asleep. Have the children who did receive an animal place it back into the bucket for the next day.

Reading Chapter Books

You can also start out rest time by reading a chapter book to them for the first 20–30 minutes.

- Read from classic books such as *Charlotte's Web* by E.B. White.
- Once every child is on his or her mat and ready, ask what the story was about, who is in the story, and what had already happened from the previous day. Then begin reading.
- Reading chapter books requires the children to remember the plot, conflict, and characters in the story.
- Pick a book that relates to your theme and that is age-appropriate. Ask the children to keep their heads on the mat and lie still while you are reading. Do allow the children to raise their hands to stop you if they do not understand what a word means.
- After you are finished reading, turn on some soft music to help drown out any outside noises. You will find that a majority of the children will be lying still and a few will already be asleep. You may need to rub or pat some of the children's backs to get some of them to sleep.

Children Who No Longer Nap

There will always be one or two children who no longer nap.

- Have a Nap Bucket for the nonsleeping children.
- Do not give the bucket to them right away. Require all children to rest for at least 30 minutes.
- Have a variety of quiet activities inside in the Nap Bucket, such as blank paper, crayons, pens, books, puzzles, playing cards, or any other small, quiet activity.
- Give the bucket to the child and have him or her play on the mat. This will eliminate the possibility of the sleeping children being awakened.

Nap Time (cont.)

Ending Nap Time

Getting the children up from resting can take some time.

- Start by allowing the children who are awake to put their napping items and mats away.
- Have these children return to the table where you have a quiet activity set out for them.
- As the children begin waking up from the classroom noise, have them put items away and join the group.
- Finally, turn on the lights.
- You will find that some children will still be able to sleep through the classroom activities. If they do, let them sleep. They probably need the rest.
- If the same child is regularly sleeping longer than the other children, place his or her mat in an individual area so you won't have to move him or her out of the way while he or she is still sleeping. Ask the parents if they would like you to wake their child up after or before a certain time. Some parents do not want their child to sleep past a certain number of hours because their child will not go to bed until late at night. Other parents will want their child to sleep as long as he or she needs.

Storing Napping Materials

Many state health departments require children's napping items to be stored separately for sanitary reasons.

- If each child has an individual cubby, show it to the parents and explain that their child can bring what he or she want for nap as long as it fits inside the cubby. This will prevent children from bringing full-size pillows and large blankets.
- If the children do not have individual cubbies, small drawstring bags that can be hung are an option. Remind parents that all napping items are to be labeled and taken home to be laundered at the end of the week.
- Resting mats that are trifold are easy to stack and store. Just remember to use a piece of tape with the child's name written on it stuck to the bottom side of the mat so the same child gets the same mat every day.
- Each Friday, all the mats will need to be sprayed and wiped down with disinfectant.

teacher tip

You can place pieces of cardboard between the folded mats, which will allow you to keep the sheets on the mats because the children's personal items will not be touching.

Posting the Schedule for the Children

You can teach children about time and the daily schedule by giving them a visual of what the day looks like.

- Provide a schedule chart hanging vertically from the door or against the wall. This can be made either by taking photos of the children engaged in activities throughout the day and placing the photos in chronological order, or you can use the reproducible pictures provided.
- Clip a clothespin on the side of the chart to indicate what is happening in the class at that moment.
- As the schedule progresses, change the clothespin to the appropriate activity. You will find that the children will refer to the schedule often. The children will begin using before, next, and after when referring to the day. This will also help you to block out activities or change one activity in the day.
- For example, you can place a black piece of paper over an activity such as outside time if the schedule has changed and the children will not be going outside because weather. If the class is going to do a cooking project instead of small group, simply place the cooking card over small-group time.
- This is a great visual reminder in addition to your verbal reminder for those children who do not like change.

Half-Day Programs

A half-day program is a center or school that has specific class times. Children who attend these programs have an established time they are to come to class at a specific time to be picked up. Often preschools that choose to have half-day programs offer an extended day or day-care option for the full-time working parents. Children in this type of program are not served lunch and do not take a nap unless staying for the extended day care.

Sample Half-Day Program Schedule

8:30–8:40	Children arrive, daily health check, students read books
8:40–8:50	Opening Circle Time, Calendar Activity, Announcements, Planning
8:50-9:45	Work Time with Open Centers/Art Table set up
9:45–9:50	Cleanup Time
9:50–10:00	Second Circle Time
10:00–11:20	Wash hands and Snack Time
10:20–11:00	Outside Time
11:00–11:15	Small-Group Time
11:15–11:30	Third Circle Time, Review, Closing song

Posting the Schedule for the Children (cont.)

Whole-Day Program

A whole-day program is a center or school that is open early in the morning and closes in the evening. Children who attend these programs often have full-time working parents who need care all day for their children. Often children are dropped off and picked up at different times throughout the day.

Whole-Day Program Schedule—Sample

7:00–8:30	Children arrive, daily health check, open work time in centers
8:30–8:40	Cleanup Time
8:40-8:50	Opening Circle Time, Calendar Activity, Announcements,
8:50–9:50	Outside Time
9:50–10:00	Circle Time/Planning
10:00–11:00	Work Time with Open Centers/Art Table set up/Open Snack set up
11:00–11:15	Small Group Time
11:15–11:45	Outside Time
11:45–12:30	Wash-Up and Lunchtime
12:30–1:00	Chapter book as children begin resting
1:00–2:30	Nap Time/Teacher Prep Time
2:30–3:00	Wake children/put resting materials away
3:00–3:15	Circle Time
3:15–3:30	Small Group Time
3:30–3:40	Snack Time
3:40–4:40	Outside Time
4:40–5:20	Planning and Work Time in Open Centers
5:20–5:30	Cleanup Time
5:30–5:40	Circle Time, Review, Closing Song
5:40–6:00	Children read books or do puzzles while waiting for parents to arrive

Posting the Schedule for the Children (cont.)

How to Make the Daily Schedule Chart

Materials Needed:

- one piece of butcher paper
- string and a wooden dowel (for the top)
- photos of the children following the schedule throughout the day
- written description of each daily event (Arrival Time, Cleanup Time, Circle Time, Work Time, Small Group, Outside Time, Snack Time, Lunchtime, Nap Time)
- rubber cement
- clothespin

How to Make:

1. Vertically lay out all the photos or the reproducible pictures vertically on the butcher paper. It is easier for the children to follow if you lay out the pictures vertically.

2. Glue the picture on the butcher paper with the corresponding description under it.

3. Laminate the chart.

4. Hang the schedule near the classroom door or in a visible spot in the classroom. Remember to move the clothespin when the class has transitioned.

5. If you are in a full-day program, have Nap Time be the last activity on the first side of the vertical chart.

6. Turn the chart over and place the afternoon schedule on the other side. This will help the children distinguish between morning and afternoon. You just need to remember to flip the chart before the children get up from their naps.

Our Schedule

Arrival Activities

Circle Time

Work Time

Snack Time

Outside Time

Schedule Cards

Arrival Activities

Circle Time

Schedule Cards (cont.)

Cleanup Time

Outside Time

#50052—*Managing an Effective Early Childhood Classroom*

Schedule Cards (cont.)

Work Time

Snack Time

Schedule Cards (cont.)

Small-Group Time

Lunchtime

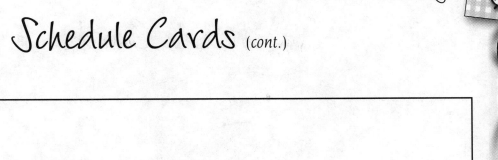

Schedule Cards (cont.)

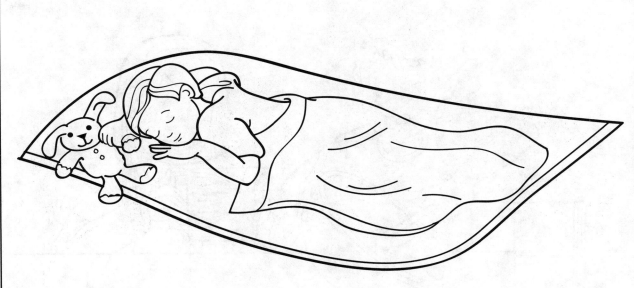

Nap Time

Wash-up Time

Schedule Cards (cont.)

Cooking Project

Music Time

Schedule Cards (cont.)

Story Time

Good-bye Time

Ending the Day

Ending Circle Time

Your last circle time of the day is a time for you and the children to reflect on what happened.

- You can pass around a beanbag or an object related to the theme, and ask the child who is holding the item to tell the class what he or she did that day. You can ask specific questions such as "What did you do inside today?" or "Tell us one thing you did outside."
- Having the children review what they did that day will help spark their memories so that when the parents ask, "What did you do at school today?" the child will have a response rather than "Nothing" or "I don't remember."
- The last thing you should do at closing circle is sing a good-bye song. End the day with fun and smiles.

After Circle Time

Parents often have a window of time in which they must pick up students from the classroom. After the last circle time, be prepared to have something for the students to do while they are waiting for their parents. For example, allow the students to play puzzles or read books. Select a task or two that is easy to clean up quickly. As parents come into the room, the parents may sit down and interact with the child as he or she completes the task and cleans up. Also, having a task for the children to work on while waiting for their parents allows you time to speak with the parents, if needed.

Before the child leaves, say good-bye and remind him or her to check the mailboxes for any information that is being sent home that day. This also provides you with an opportunity to speak with the parents to let them know about any important information.

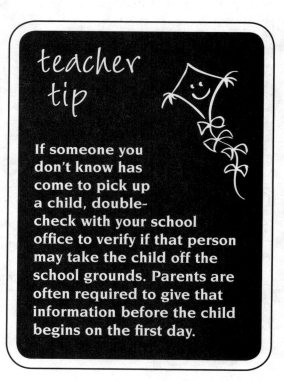

teacher tip

If someone you don't know has come to pick up a child, double-check with your school office to verify if that person may take the child off the school grounds. Parents are often required to give that information before the child begins on the first day.

Informing Parents of the Day's Events

Parent communication is essential for creating a relationship between you and the parents. Have a parent board on the outside of your classroom or close to the sign-in/out sheets. This can be a corkboard or a dry-erase board. At the end of the day, post a short note to the parents stating, in educational terms, what activities took place that day. It can explain your small-group activity or something the class did at Circle Time. For example, "Today we brainstormed and made a list of all the items we will need if we go camping. Next we sorted the items into categories. The categories were: Cooler, Suitcase, Cooking Box, and Other Supplies." Leaving a note telling the parents about an activity the class did is a great way for the parents to begin a conversation with their child in the car on the way home.

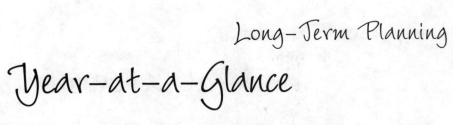

Year-at-a-Glance

Looking ahead and planning for the year in an early childhood classroom is simple. Young children learn best when they are given meaningful hands-on experiences. Activities and gatherings in your community are things that the children will be exposed to. Take a calendar and mark down what important events are happening in the community for that particular month. Talking about spring in November does not have meaning to the children and they will not be able to relate. Mapping out the year the first time will require some research and time, but after that, you can keep the record as a template and just change the dates.

Holidays

A great place to start is mapping out the holidays and months that are devoted to a specific theme every year. For example, Fire Prevention week is in October. Take the following yearly chart and start with the beginning of your academic calendar. Remember to include multicultural days such as Rosh Hashanah, Yom Kippur, Hanukkah, Ramadan, Chinese New Year, Black History Month, Passover, Easter, Christmas, Kwanzaa, and Cinco de Mayo.

Themes That Relate to One Another

Keep themes that relate to one another close together so they can flow from one month into the next. For example, gardening is a good way to get the children outside and looking for things in the environment. If the study of insects is the next theme, this is an easy flow from one subject into another.

Getting Materials for Your Themes

Local stores will donate materials if they receive letters from you stating what the class needs and how the class plans on using the materials. Tree and flower donations for your planting theme may take some time on your part, but the children and parents will benefit from the experience.

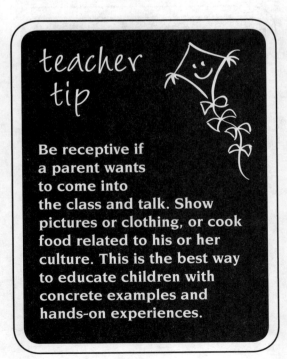

teacher tip

Be receptive if a parent wants to come into the class and talk. Show pictures or clothing, or cook food related to his or her culture. This is the best way to educate children with concrete examples and hands-on experiences.

Year-at-a-Glance (cont.)

Community Events

Each community will also have particular events happening each month. Pay close attention to your neighborhood and be creative in ways in which you can get your class involved in the community. Community events that are happening in San Diego, California, in March are going to be completely different than the events that are happening in Denver, Colorado. So, look at the needs and interests of the children in your class. Look for community events in your local newspaper or family magazine that is distributed in the community. Some of these published pieces will have a day-by-day calendar of public events for the month. For example, Arbor Day is April 10. Research the history of Nebraska and Arbor Day. Have the class draw pictures of trees. Have the children dictate a letter to a local store or public official and ask if the class can plant a tree on that specific day or week.

Other Dates to Include

Other great dates to incorporate into your curriculum are the first days of the seasons, Mickey Mouse's birthday, Dr. Seuss's birthday, Johnny Appleseed's birthday, Poetry Day, and Earth Day.

Month-by-Month

Take the experiences and feelings of the children into consideration when planning month-by-month. After you have planned out the year, remember to be flexible—nothing is set in stone.

teacher tip

Use a separate Month-by-Month Planning Sheet to write down all the children's birthdays.

If you have Farm Animals planned for the first week in May and a child brings in a tadpole that week, you will need to adjust your entire schedule. The children will be looking, thinking, and talking about tadpoles and frogs. You will need to change your plans to incorporate the theme of frogs. If you don't adjust your plans, an educational moment is lost. If you are in a year-round school, the summer themes should require children to be outside. Plan field trips to keep the children out in the community and enjoying summer. Mapping out the year is a guideline for what you want to focus on. Pages 145–147 provide some suggestions of themes or areas of focus for the months of the year.

Month-by-Month

Use these topics to fill in the months in which you feel they will work best.

September

Getting to Know Me, I Am a Can-Do Kid

- Having the children talk about themselves allows you to get to know them and their families, and allows them to talk about something they know really well: themselves. Encourage an I-can-do attitude by having the children talk about, draw, and share all the things they can do.

October

Fall, Fire Prevention, Halloween and Safety, National Popcorn Week

- The month starts out with Fire Prevention, which is an important topic. Bring in firefighters as guest speakers, talk about fire safety, and practice "Stop, Drop, and Roll."
- October is the first month in the school year with a holiday: Halloween. Keep in mind that some religions do not celebrate Halloween, so remember to be sensitive.

November

Native Americans, What I Am Thankful For, Manners, National Book Week

November is an excellent way of bringing in multicultural experiences and to encourage the children to think of all the things for which they are thankful. It is also a good opportunity for them to learn and practice table manners.

- You may want to plan your first parent involvement event by having a potluck feast with all the families in your class.

December

Winter, Holidays Around the World

- December is full of multicultural experiences for the children, wonderful music, and lots of creative art experiences.
- One way of having the children participate in the season of giving is by having a Gently Used Book Party. On a specific day, have each child bring a gift-wrapped, used book in good condition. Start by randomly drawing each child's name and have him or her choose a book that is in the pile. Remind them that they may not choose the book they brought. Then, all together have the children open the books they picked.
- Cooking with the children in December is a must. There are so many multicultural dishes that can be made by the children.

Month-by-Month (cont.)

January

New Year's, Animals That Live in the Snow and Hibernating Animals, Martin Luther King Jr. Day

- In January, studying animals in the snow and animals that hibernate is a good way of incorporating geography and habitat.
- Celebrate Martin Luther King Jr. Day by discussing how important it is to be kind to one another. Discuss with the children how they are the same as and how they are different from one another. This is a holiday to celebrate being human.

February

Groundhog Day, Valentine's Day, Presidents' Day, and Feelings

- February is a good month to talk about feelings, which connects well with Valentine's Day.
- This is also a good month to incorporate people in the neighborhood, such as the mail carrier.

March

Dr. Seuss's Birthday, Farm Animals, Zoo Animals, Saint Patrick's Day

- Dr. Seuss's birthday is in the first week of March. The children enjoy rhymes and the rhythms in Dr. Seuss books. Talking about being an author is appropriate at this time.
- Discussing farm animals in the spring allows you to have small farm animals (ducks, chicks, bunnies, and lambs) bought to the school, or you may take the children on a field trip to a farm to observe baby animals.

April

Spring, Planting a Garden, April Fool's Day, Easter

- Depending on where you live, March or April is a perfect month to plant a garden. Look on the back of the pack of seeds you wish to plant and see when the best time to plant is. This takes planning ahead.

May

Insects, Mother's Day

- Talking about insects right after planting the garden is an easy transition. The children will need to take care of the garden until the fall. Have the children go outside and look for things such as insects in the outside environment.

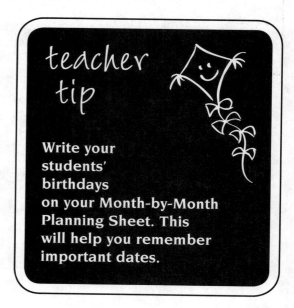

teacher tip

Write your students' birthdays on your Month-by-Month Planning Sheet. This will help you remember important dates.

Month-by-Month (cont.)

June

Transportation, Father's Day

- There are many different forms of transportation, some of which you may not have in your town. Remember to include subways, boats, trains, and other forms of transportation that the children may not be familiar with.

July

Summer, Independence Day, Ocean Animals

- July is a month for the children to explore summer. Having red, white, and blue activities along with an emphasis on America is always fun for the children. The class will be able to relate easily to what they will be seeing in the community.
- Encourage water play with the theme of ocean animals.

August

Camping, Getting Ready for a New School or Teacher

- Camping and vacations are easy themes to incorporate with August.
- This month will be the last month you will have most of these children in your class. Kindergarten will be their next step. Preparing the children for the next adventure is crucial to ensure that they are comfortable moving on. These children are going on to kindergarten and to the unknown. Help the children work through any fears or questions they may have. You may want to contact a local kindergarten teacher to come in and tell the children about what comes next.

Other topics you might like to focus on throughout the year are

- Colors
- Numbers
- Nursery rhymes
- Weather
- Bubbles
- Dinosaurs
- Frogs
- Body parts
- Nutrition
- Community helpers

Month-by-Month (cont.)

Month-by-Month Planning Sheet—Sample

Month	Theme/Areas of Focus
September	• Getting to Know Me • I Am a Can-Do Kid
October	• Fall • Fire Prevention • Halloween • Safety • National Popcorn Week
November	• Native Americans • What I Am Thankful For • Manners • National Book Week
December	• Winter • Holidays Around the World
January	• New Year's Day • Animals That Live in the Snow and Hibernating Animals • Martin Luther King Jr. Day
February	• Groundhog Day • Valentine's Day • Presidents' Day • Feelings
March	• Farm Animals • Zoo Animals • Saint Patrick's Day
April	• Spring • Planting a Garden • April Fool's Day
May	• Insects • Mother's Day
June	• Transportation • Father's Day
July	• Summer • Independence Day • Ocean Animals
August	• Camping • Getting Reading for a New School Year or Teacher

Month-by-Month (cont.)

Month-by-Month Planning Sheet—Master

Month	Theme/Areas of Focus
September	
October	
November	
December	
January	
February	
March	
April	
May	
June	
July	
August	

Short-Term Planning
A Peek at the Week

When looking at the week, or even a day in your classroom, many factors need to be considered. Reading out loud every day, planning activities that meet the pre-K standards, developing a curriculum around a theme, and keeping school fun can be confusing, and at times difficult. Start by breaking down the month into weeks.

- Take the monthly plan and figure out how to break it down into weeks.
- Decide what will be the focus for each week of each month.
- When beginning with the first week, make a list of all the materials, books, and lesson plans you have available that relate to the weekly topic.
- Next, write down all the activities (music, language, art, math) that relate to the weekly topic. Many curriculum books are available for ideas and lesson plans. When deciding on the read-aloud books or literature that you are going to have available, you may want to visit your local library.
- When planning your curriculum, consider the standards that are set for pre-K children so that you can incorporate activities that will meet those standards.
- The standards are broken down into categories. These categories are Arts, Economics, Health, History, Language Arts, Life Skills, Working with Others, Mathematics, and Physical Education.

Once you have the themes for the weeks, fill in the Weekly Outline.

- Start with a read-aloud book.
- Incorporate the activities around the book. This will create continuity and a flow to the day.

Planning Example for April—Planting Our Garden

Week One:	Planning a Garden. What will we plant? Where will we plant? How do we get the area ready?
Week Two:	Planting and taking care of the garden.
Week Three:	Measuring and continuing to take care of the garden.
Week Four:	Things we can make with what we are growing in our garden and continue measuring the growth of the plants.

teacher tip

Many libraries will not only have a wide selection of materials available but may also have prop boxes associated with your theme.

A Peek at the Week — Sample

Weekly Outline: Week One

Theme: Planning a Garden

Read Aloud Books:

1. *Round the Garden* by Omri Glasir

2. *Our Silly Garden* by Karen Berman Nagel

3. *The Surprise Garden* by Zoe Hall

4. *Over in the Garden* by Jennifer Ward

5. *Growing Colors* by Bruce McMillan

Math Activities:

1. Sort what fruits, vegetables, or flowers grow above, on, and under the ground.
2. Count different kinds of seeds. Sort by small, medium, and large.

Science Activities:

1. Carnation stem cut and put into two different glasses of colored water.
2. Try to grow a sweet potato or an avocado.

Music Activity:

1. "Each of Us Is a Flower" by Charlotte Diamond (Found reference here: http://www.songsforteaching.com/charlottediamond/eachofusisaflower.htm)

Economics or Community Awareness:

1. Take a field trip to the farmer's market.

Other:

1. Guest Speaker: a botanist

Art Activities:

1. Window-paint a garden

2. Paint with flowers

3. Seed collage

4. Draw a picture of what our garden will look like

5. Potato prints

Language Activities:

1. Document each child's language as he or she draws in a gardening journal.

2 Positional activity with strawberry baskets

Cooking Activity:

1. Make guacamole and nachos.

Weekly Outline: Week _____

Theme: Planning a Garden

Read Aloud Books:

1. _____
2. _____
3. _____
4. _____
5. _____

Art Activities:

1. _____
2. _____
3. _____
4. _____
5. _____

Math Activities:

1. _____
2. _____

Language Activities:

1. _____
2. _____

Science Activities:

1. _____
2. _____

Cooking Activities:

1. _____
2. _____

Music Activity:

1. _____

Economics or Community Awareness:

1. _____

Other:

1. _____

What Today Brings

Once you have the Weekly Outline filled in, the next step is to fill in the Weekly Plan. The weekly plan breaks the day into the specific time you have devoted to a specific activity. When filling in the lesson plan, keep activities that relate to one another on the same day. For example, if the class is going to make guacamole and nachos, this is a good day to have the avocado pit as the science focus for small group.

Laying out Activities

Space big activities apart. For example, the guest speaker should be at the beginning of the unit and a field trip to the farmer's market should be at the end of the unit. This will keep the class from becoming overwhelmed and will not upset children who have a difficult time adjusting to change in the daily routine.

The Weekly Outline

If you teach in a full-day program, you will fill out two Weekly Plans, one for the morning class time and one for the afternoon class. If you work in a half-day program, you will just fill out one Weekly Plan. When filling in your lesson plan, you may not use all the ideas in the outline, but filling in all the spaces will allow you more choices and greater flexibility to move activities around.

The Lesson Plan

As you fill in the Weekly Lesson Plan, think of the objective for each activity.

- Use at least one activity from each category when filling in the Weekly Lesson Plan. This will ensure that you have a variety of activities and will also avoid having only math or only language activities in the week.
- Once you have a routine established—for example, every Wednesday the class will do a cooking activity—filling in the lesson plan will be quick and easy. By making a master copy of your weekly plan, you will not have to fill in all the activities that repeat daily, and it will shorten the amount of time you spend on writing plans.
- An example of an activity that is done daily is the Calendar. The Calendar activity will be done at the same time and in the same order every day. Activities that will change daily are Circle Times and Small Group Times.

teacher tip

Create your own lesson plan book by photocopying the master Weekly Plan that meets your needs. Three-hole punch the pages and place them in a binder.

What Today Brings (cont.)

Weekly Plan for a Half-Day Program

Weekly Lesson Plan

For the Week of _____ Theme: _____

	Monday	Tuesday	Wednesday	Thursday	Friday
8:30–8:40—Children arrive, daily health check, students read books					
8:40–8:50—Opening Circle Time, Calendar Activity, Announcements					
8:50–9:45—Work Time					
8:45–9:50—Cleanup Time					
9:50–10:00—Second Circle Time					
10:00–10:20—Wash hands and Snack Time					
10:20–11:00—Outside Time					
11:00–11:15—Small-Group Time					
11:15 – 11:30—Third Circle Time, review, closing song					

What Today Brings (cont.)

Weekly Plan for a Full-Day Program (cont.)

Weekly Lesson Plan

For the Week of _____ Theme: _____

	Monday	Tuesday	Wednesday	Thursday	Friday
7:00–8:30—Children arrive, daily health check, open work time in centers					
8:30–8:40—Cleanup Time					
8:40–8:50—Opening Circle Time including Calendar Activity and Announcements					
8:50–9:50—Outside Time					
9:50–10:00—Circle Time					
10:00–11:00—Work Time in Open Centers/Art Table/ Open Snack					
11:00–11:15—Small Group Time					
11:15 – 11:45—Outside Time					
11:45–12:30—Wash up and Lunch Time					
12:30 – 1:00—Chapter Book as children begin resting					

#50052—*Managing an Effective Early Childhood Classroom*

What Today Brings (cont.)

Weekly Plan for a Full-Day Program (cont.)

Weekly Lesson Plan

For the Week of _____   Theme: _____

	Monday	Tuesday	Wednesday	Thursday	Friday
1:00–2:30 —Nap Time/ Teacher Prep Time					
2:30–3:00 —Wake children/Put resting materials away					
3:00–3:15 —Circle Time					
3:15–3:30 —Small Group Time					
3:30–3:40 —Snack Time					
3:40–4:40 —Outside Time					
4:40–5:20 —Planning and Work Time in Open Centers					
5:20–5:30 —Cleanup Time					
5:30–5:40 —Circle Time, Review, Closing song					
5:40–6:00 —Children read books or do puzzles while waiting for parents to arrive					

Planning Field Trips

Getting your class outside the classroom and giving the children opportunities to have hands-on experiences in the community is what field trips are all about. Often, preschool classes do not take many field trips because of safety reasons, or because the teacher and parents may not feel comfortable taking the children off the school grounds. If you have enough parents who support you in providing educational, hands-on experiences and you give them enough advance notice of a planned field trip, taking the children on field trips will be easy. Use the community and its resources for field trips as much as possible. These field trips are meaningful and provide the children with hands-on experiences.

Deciding Where to Go

Look at your long-term planning sheet. Brainstorm all the places in your town you could visit each month, no matter the distance or cost. Then decide which trips would have the most meaningful experience for the children.

List of Neighborhood Field Trips

- Grocery store
- Pumpkin patch
- Doctor's office
- Farmers market
- Zoo

- Bakery
- Library
- Fire station
- Ice cream parlor
- Museums

- Pizza parlor
- Pet store
- Florist
- Police office
- Garden/hardware store

- Post office
- Dentist office
- Veterinarian's office
- Local park

teacher tip

Take the class out on a field trip a minimum of four times a year, once a quarter. Children learn a tremendous amount about the world by going on field trips.

Planning Field Trips (cont.)

Theme-Related Trips

Relate your field trips to the themes the class is currently studying. In this way, information students have been learning is reinforced on the field trip. For example, this month, you are talking about transportation. A class in California could take a public bus to a trolley station, then get on a boat that goes near the airport. By participating in this field trip, the children would ride on four different forms of transportation. Along the way, you could have the children look for more forms of transportation, such as people riding bikes, skateboarding, rollerblading, and walking. Be creative in planning where to take the children.

Making Arrangements

- Once you have decided where you would like to go, the next step is choosing a date.
- Look at your calendar and call the location that you would like to visit to make arrangements.
- When you call the location, be specific about how many children and the times that you will arrive and leave, and ask the total cost.
- You should plan at least 30 days in advance. This allows enough time for parents to request the time off from work to volunteer for the field trip.
- Remember to put the field trip notice in both the monthly newsletter and in the monthly calendar. Have a volunteer sign-up sheet available.
- You will also need each child's parents to sign a permission slip allowing you to take their child off the school grounds.

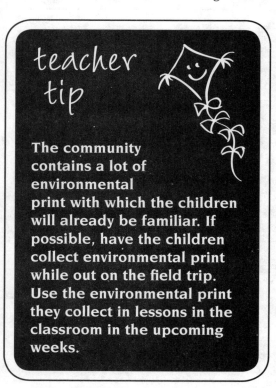

teacher tip

The community contains a lot of environmental print with which the children will already be familiar. If possible, have the children collect environmental print while out on the field trip. Use the environmental print they collect in lessons in the classroom in the upcoming weeks.

Getting to the Location?

- Having the parents drive is an excellent way to get the children to the location if you have enough drivers. You will need a signed permission slip for each child who will be riding in someone else's car other than his or her parent's car. Each child will be required to be in a car seat.
- If you choose to take public transportation, children five and under usually ride free and no car seats are required. Call your local public transportation office for bus numbers and times.
- If the final location is only a few blocks from your school, walking is always fun and great exercise.
- Your last option is to rent a bus. This option is expensive, but no car seats are required and all the children can go together at the same time.

Planning Field Trips (cont.)

Bus Permission Slip

_____ has my permission to go on a field trip by bus
         (Child's Name)

with his/her class on _____ to _____.
                 (Date)   (Destination)

My signature gives _____ my permission
                       (School Name)

to provide any emergency care deemed necessary.

Numbers where I can be reached: _____ or _____

Date _____ Parent's Signature _____

Planning Field Trips (cont.)

Private Car Permission Slip

_____ has my permission to go on a field trip by
(Child's Name)

private transportation with his/her class on _____
(Date)

to _____.
(Destination)

My signature gives _____ my permission
(School Name)

to provide any emergency care deemed necessary.

Numbers where I can be reached: _____ or _____

Date _____ Parent's Signature _____

Planning Field Trips (cont.)

Walking Field Trip

_____ has my permission to go on a walking field
        (Child's Name)

trip with his/her class on _____
                            (Date)

to _____.
             (Destination)

My signature gives _____ my permission to provide
                     (School Name)

any emergency care deemed necessary.

Numbers where I can be reached: _____ or _____

Date _____ Parent's Signature _____

Just a Reminder

Our class will be going on a field trip on _____ .

We are getting there by _____ .

We are going to leave the school at _____ .

We will be returning by _____ .

The cost is _____ .

Permission slips and money need to be returned to me by _____ .

I will need _____ volunteers. Please let me know as soon as possible if you can attend the field trip with the class.

Remember to have your child:

- eat a healthy breakfast.
- use sunblock.
- wear appropriate shoes and clothes.

Thank you,

_____
(Teacher's Signature)

Planning Field Trips (cont.)

Sign-Up Sheet for Volunteers

Destination: _____

Time the class is leaving: _____

Approximate return time: _____

Transportation: Private Automobile

Transportation: Private Automobile		
Parent's Name	Driving (write Yes or No)	Number of Passengers

Planning Field Trips (cont.)

Sign-Up Sheet for Volunteers

Destination: _____

Time the class is leaving: _____

Approximate return time: _____

Transportation: Walking or bus (circle one)

Parent's Name:

_____

_____

_____

_____

_____

_____

_____

_____

_____

_____

_____

_____

_____

Planning Field Trips (cont.)

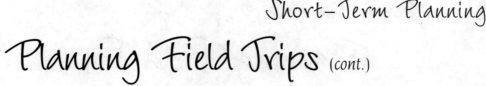

Checklist for Field Trip

Field Trip to _____		
Child's Name	Permission Slip	Paid: _____ (insert amount)

Planning Field Trips (cont.)

Adult-Child Ratio on Field Trips

The best adult-child ratio for field trips is one-to-one or even one adult to two children. If you have great parent involvement, these ratios will be possible, but don't count on it for every field trip. Having one adult to four children is a good ratio for effective supervision and you will probably be able to count on enough parents to volunteer.

Preparing the Children for the Field Trip

Preparing the children for a field trip is essential to having a successful event.

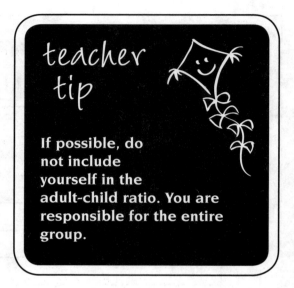

teacher tip

If possible, do not include yourself in the adult-child ratio. You are responsible for the entire group.

- Mark the date of the field trip on your classroom calendar and explain what they will be doing when they get there. For example, if you are going to the pizza parlor, explain that each one of the children will need to pay attention to the instructions of the manager because they are each going to make an individual pizza for lunch.
- On the day of the field trip, explain again where they are going, what they will be doing, and what behaviors you expect to see.
- The more field trips you take the children on, the more accustomed to the expectations and the adjustment in the daily schedule they will become.

Children look forward to field trips because they enjoy the adventure of something new and they benefit from hands-on experiences.

The Day of the Field Trip

On the day of the field trip, you will already have a list of the parents who are volunteering and the number of children who have turned in the money and signed permission slips. You will need to put nametags on all the children, pack a bag, and assign the children to the responsible adults.

Planning Field Trips (cont.)

Name Tags

On each tag, you will need to put the name of the school and the school phone number. This will allow an adult to call the school and inform the school if a child is lost. Do not put the child's name on the name tag because this will allow a stranger to call a child by name and to coax the child away from the group by trying to convince the child that he or she knows him or her. You can use large label stickers, masking tape, or hanging name tags. If you choose to use stickers or masking tape, place it on the center of the children's backs. This way, they cannot pull them off. If you are planning a lot of field trips, consider creating hanging name tags.

Hanging Name Tags

- Use the following pattern, and write the school name and phone number on it.
- Laminate all the labels.
- Next, use a hole punch to punch a hole at the top for the rubber band to go through.
- As the children arrive the morning of the field trip, attach the name tag by sticking the rubber band through the hole at the top of the tag and through a belt loop, a strap on the child's shirt, or any other loop you can find. Then, take the name tag through the other end loop of the rubber band.
- This is an easy way to make reusable name tags. You can also use a large safety pin and pin the name tags to the children.

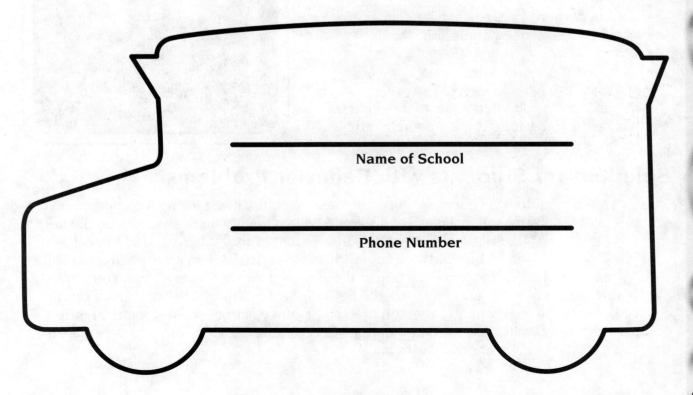

Name of School

Phone Number

Planning Field Trips (cont.)

Assigning Children to Parents in Advance

If planning in advance, you will have a list of all names of the children that each parent will be responsible for.

- Each parent should be given a list of the children he or she is responsible for. For example: Mrs. Hill (Matt's Mom): Matt, Jenny, Chris, Sarah.
- Just before you are about to leave, ask the children who have parents attending the field trip to stand and walk over to their parent.
- Then you will tell each child to stand as you read his or her name.
- Explain that those children will be going with a classmate's mom or dad. Send them to stand with that parent.
- Giving the volunteers written lists of the children they are responsible for will help them remember the children's names.

Assigning children to a specific group and parent will allow you to make sure that certain combinations of children are split up.

Items You Need to Take with You

Before you leave the school grounds, there are some items you will need to take with you. The items can be carried in a backpack or a tote bag.

- A cell phone
- Parent emergency numbers
- Parent consent for medical emergency
- Each child's signed permission slip
- Plastic gloves
- First-aid kit
- Tissue
- A list of all the children going on the field trip
- Depending how long you are planning to be gone, a small snack for the children.

teacher tip

Pack a unisex change of clothes just in case a child has an accident.

Solutions for Students with Behavior Problems

Safety of all the children is your most important responsibility when taking the children off the school site. If for any reason you feel a child would be in danger if he or she went on the field trip, you have two options. You can either require a parent of the child to attend the field trip with you, or you can leave the child at school with another class. When approaching the child's parents, explain that this is not a reflection of the child but rather a safety issue. You want the child to have a positive experience on the field trip just like rest of the class. You simply cannot afford to have all your attention on their child; it needs to be focused on the entire group. Most parents will make accommodations to go on the field trip, but if for any reason they can't, leave the child at school with another class.

Monthly Newsletter

Parents are your best allies, and parent communication can make all the difference in your class. Parents want to be included in their children's education, and making them feel part of the educational process will encourage participation. In today's society, families often require both parents to be in the workforce, leaving many children in full-time preschools or in day care. It is important to remember that these parents want be an active part of their child's education just as much as does the stay-at-home mom or dad. In addition to speaking to the parents daily when they bring their children to class, sending home monthly newsletters, calendars, Accident Reports, OOPS Reports, and posting daily notes and lesson plans will keep the parents informed.

At the end of the month, you should send out a classroom newsletter for the upcoming month. For some parents, this will be the only form of communication between you and them. It is important to let the parents know what is going on. When a parent asks a child, "What did you do at school today?" the child will almost always say, "Nothing" or "I can't remember." By providing a newsletter and calendar, the parents can ask specific questions, such as "How was the banana bread you made today, and what ingredients did you use?" The newsletter should have different sections and be quick and easy to read. Some section suggestions are: Looking Ahead, Special Reminders, I Need Help, and Thank You.

Looking Ahead

Looking Ahead is the section where you list the dates and themes for each week. This will let the parents know what the theme, letter, or topics will be for each week of the month.

I Need Help

The I Need Help area can be for anything, from asking for recyclable items like soda bottles to requesting drivers for a field trip. Do not be afraid to ask for help.

Special Reminders

Special Reminders is the section where you may list any visitors, guest speakers, field trips, birthdays, class parties, and days when the school will be closed.

Thank You

Keep track of anything that you need to say thank you for. If a parent comes into the class and reads a story, brings in empty baby food jars, volunteers, or brings in a snack for the children, always write a thank-you note and post it in your newsletter.

Monthly Newsletter (cont.)

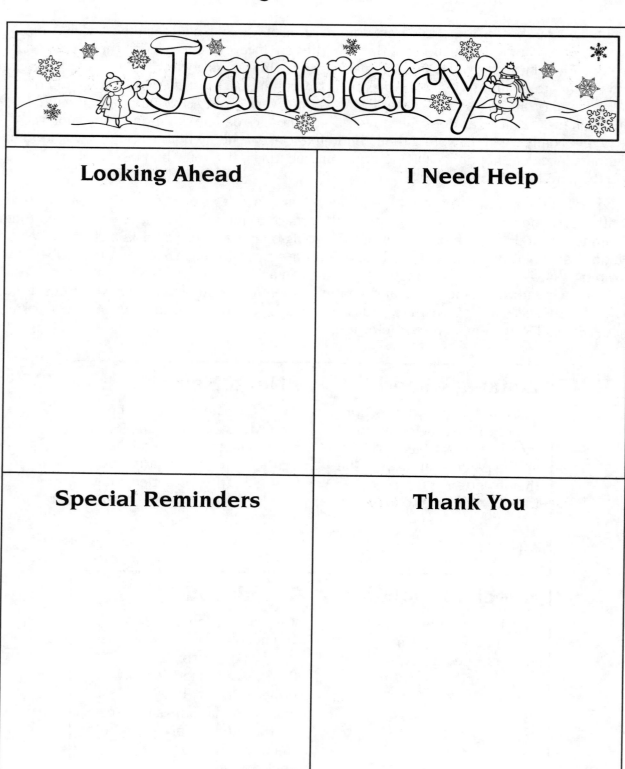

Looking Ahead

I Need Help

Special Reminders

Thank You

Monthly Newsletter (cont.)

Looking Ahead	I Need Help
Special Reminders	**Thank You**

Monthly Newsletter (cont.)

Looking Ahead	I Need Help

Special Reminders	Thank You

Monthly Newsletter (cont.)

April

Looking Ahead	I Need Help
Special Reminders	**Thank You**

Monthly Newsletter (cont.)

Looking Ahead	I Need Help
Special Reminders	**Thank You**

Monthly Newsletter (cont.)

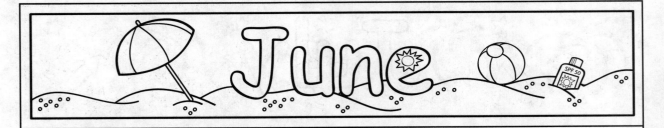

Looking Ahead	I Need Help
Special Reminders	**Thank You**

Monthly Newsletter (cont.)

Looking Ahead	I Need Help
Special Reminders	**Thank You**

Monthly Newsletter (cont.)

Looking Ahead	I Need Help

Special Reminders	Thank You

Monthly Newsletter (cont.)

Looking Ahead

I Need Help

Special Reminders

Thank You

#50052—*Managing an Effective Early Childhood Classroom*

Monthly Newsletter (cont.)

Looking Ahead	**I Need Help**
Special Reminders	**Thank You**

Monthly Newsletter (cont.)

November

Looking Ahead	**I Need Help**
Special Reminders	**Thank You**

Monthly Newsletter (cont.)

Looking Ahead	I Need Help
Special Reminders	**Thank You**

Monthly Calendar

The monthly calendar is a repeat of the newsletter only in calendar form with additional information. By giving a calendar, the parents can add in or change any additional event that may have come up. Encourage the parents to post the calendar on the refrigerator where it will be visible on a daily basis.

Laying out the Month on the Calendar

Highlight any event or activity that requires special attention by circling or putting squiggly lines around the day. This is also a perfect place for you to put what the child should bring each week for Share Day and what the children will be cooking. These are not written in the newsletter. Include as much as you can about what will be happening in your class.

Educational Terms

Include educational terms like counting, sorting, listing, observing, drawing, demonstrating, singing, experimenting, and mixing in your newsletter. This allows the parent to see the types of skills their child is learning, as well as which prekindergarten standards are being met. Give the parents both the newsletter and the monthly calendar together.

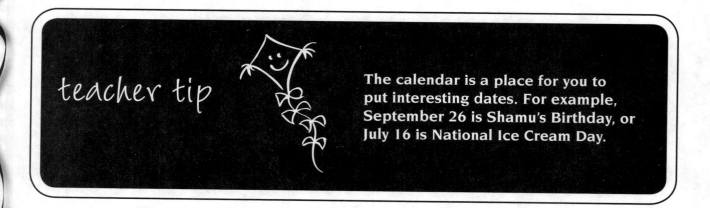

teacher tip

The calendar is a place for you to put interesting dates. For example, September 26 is Shamu's Birthday, or July 16 is National Ice Cream Day.

Monthly Calendar (cont.)

Monday	Tuesday	Wednesday	Thursday	Friday

Monthly Calendar (cont.)

February

Monday	Tuesday	Wednesday	Thursday	Friday

Parent Communication

Monthly Calendar (cont.)

Monday	Tuesday	Wednesday	Thursday	Friday

© Shell Education   #50052—Managing an Effective Early Childhood Classroom   185

Monthly Calendar (cont.)

Monday	Tuesday	Wednesday	Thursday	Friday

#50052—*Managing an Effective Early Childhood Classroom*

Monthly Calendar (cont.)

Monday	Tuesday	Wednesday	Thursday	Friday

Monthly Calendar (cont.)

Monday	Tuesday	Wednesday	Thursday	Friday

Monthly Calendar (cont.)

Monday	Tuesday	Wednesday	Thursday	Friday

Monthly Calendar (cont.)

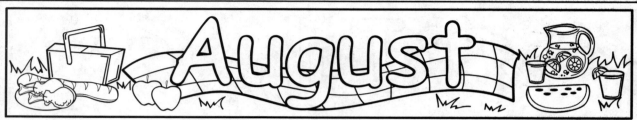

Monday	Tuesday	Wednesday	Thursday	Friday

#50052—*Managing an Effective Early Childhood Classroom* © *Shell Education*

Monthly Calendar (cont.)

Monday	Tuesday	Wednesday	Thursday	Friday

Monthly Calendar (cont.)

Monday	Tuesday	Wednesday	Thursday	Friday

Monthly Calendar (cont.)

Monday	Tuesday	Wednesday	Thursday	Friday

Monthly Calendar (cont.)

Monday	Tuesday	Wednesday	Thursday	Friday

Keeping Parents Informed

Accidents

Accidents will naturally occur in any environment where children are encouraged to take risks. When a child is injured in your class, it is your responsibility to inform the parents.

Documenting Accidents

Always document any injury in a notebook with the date and time, who was involved, what happened, and what care was given to the child. This is for you or the school to refer back to if there is ever a question.

When to Call the Parents

- If a child is injured on the head or face, no matter how small the injury, call the parents. They will appreciate the effort and it only takes a few moments of your time. Parents may become concerned if they see a scratch across their child's face and they were not contacted.
- When you talk to the parent, the first thing you should do is reassure them that their child is all right. Any time a parent gets a call from their child's school, they will naturally assume the worst.
- Explain to the parents what activity the child was involved in, how he or she was hurt, and what you did. For example, "Hello, Mr. Smith this is Mrs. Marshall, Johnny's teacher. Johnny is fine. I just wanted to call and let you know he has a scratch across the left side of his face. He was looking for worms, and when he stood up, the branch from the tree scratched his face. We washed it off with water and put a bandage on it. He also asked for some ice. I will attach an accident report to his backpack."
- If the situation involved another child, do not tell the parent who it was. That is confidential and you don't need the parent calling the other parents about what happened. Simply explain, "Johnny was playing with another child, digging for worms using shovels. When the other child became excited about finding a worm, his shovel scratched Johnny's left cheek."
- If you feel the child needs medical attention, calmly explain why. For example, "Johnny was digging for worms with another child. The other child was using a stick and accidentally scratched Johnny across the face when he became excited. I washed it off and have put a bandage on it. It looks pretty deep and you might want to take Johnny to the doctor to see if he needs stitches."

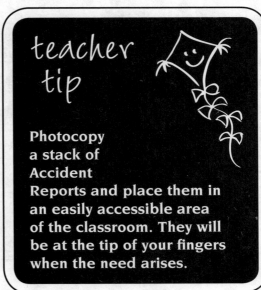

teacher tip

Photocopy a stack of Accident Reports and place them in an easily accessible area of the classroom. They will be at the tip of your fingers when the need arises.

Keeping Parents Informed (cont.)

Accident Report Form—Sample

Child's Name: <u>Graciela Ewing</u>   Date: <u>September 25</u>

Nature/Cause of Injury: <u>Graciela was jumping on the balance beam and fell off</u>

<u>and banged her knee.</u>

_____

Action Taken: <u>An ice pack was applied to Graciela's knee. She said she felt better</u>

<u>and didn't need the ice pack any longer.</u>

_____

Parents Contacted: <u>No</u>   Sent to Nurse: <u>No</u>

Accident Report Form

Child's Name: _____ Date: _____

Nature/Cause of Injury: _____

_____

_____

Action Taken: _____

_____

_____

Parents Contacted: _____   Sent to Nurse: _____

Keeping Parents Informed (cont.)

OOPS Report

A report that refers to a toileting accident is sometimes called an OOPS report.
- On this report, state what the child was doing and what happened.
- Write on the note to the parents if the child was just too busy playing and didn't want to stop, if he or she was right in front of the toilet, or sleeping at naptime.
- If toileting accidents occur often with the same child, keep notes on the time of day, how much the child is drinking, or if the child is complaining of any discomfort.
- The parents will want to know if they need to speak to the child's doctor.

Getting Information to the Parents

Communicating with parents is essential in creating a home-school relationship. Getting information from you to the parent can be difficult if you do not see the parents on a daily basis. If the school you work at has before- and after-class day care or if you are employed at an all-day school, children will be dropped off before you get there and often stay after you have left for the day.

Parent Information Center

Create a central location for communication, such as near the entrance of the classroom or where the parent will be required to sign the child out. This area can be called your parent information center.

- In this center, you will have your daily lesson plans posted or the "What We Did Today" note, your sign in/out sheets, and any special notes for upcoming events.
- On your parent information board, you can also include any interesting articles from magazines or the newspaper that you think your families may be interested in.
- You may also want to include your mailboxes.

Keeping Parents Informed (cont.)

OOPS Report Form—Sample

Child's Name: <u>**Beatrix Smith**</u>   Date: <u>**September 25**</u>

Nature/Cause of Injury: <u>**Beatrix was sleeping very soundly during nap time and**</u>

<u>**wet her pants.**</u>

_____

Action Taken: <u>**Beatrix changed into her dry set of clothes. The wet clothes were**</u>

<u>**placed into a plastic grocery bag to be taken home by Beatrix.**</u>

_____

Parents Contacted: <u>**Yes. When reviewing the previous OOPS reports on Beatrix,**</u> I

<u>**let the parents know that she might need to be evaluated by her doctor as she**</u> has

<u>**many more accidents than the other children.**</u>

Sent to Nurse: <u>**No**</u>

OOPS Report Form

Child's Name: _____ Date: _____

Nature/Cause of Injury: _____

_____

_____

Action Taken: _____

_____

_____

Parents Contacted: _____

_____

_____

Sent to Nurse: _____

Getting Information to the Parents

Mailboxes

Create a separate mailbox for each child or family in your class. This will give you a spot to place important information and a specific place for the parents to look. By creating a family mailbox, you will be able to get information to the parents and see which family has not picked up any important information. A family mailbox is an effective way to get your monthly newsletters, calendars, reports, and any other special notes home. You can make these using different methods.

Bottle or Milk-Carton Mailboxes

The first method is to use either a two-liter bottle or a half-gallon milk carton for each family, with the top cut off. Allow the children to decorate a piece of paper (stickers, paint, markers, etc.) that will be used to wrap their family's mailbox. Next make sure the child's name is on the mailbox and glue all mailboxes together, side-by-side.

Hanging Shoe Rack Mailbox

The next method in creating a family mailbox is to use an over-the-door shoe rack. This can be hung over the door, or you can nail it to the wall. You will need enough slots for every child or family. Place the child's name or picture on the outside of the slot to create an individual mail slot.

Backpacks

If your school requires the children to bring a backpack each day, you can always place information in it or staple it on the outside of the child's bag. Take the special note and wrap it around the shoulder strap and staple the two ends of the paper together. Do not staple it into the backpack as it might create a hole. The problem with putting information inside the backpack or on the outside of the backpack is that you don't get the opportunity to see if the parent received the information. The note can get ripped off or shoved to the bottom of the bag.

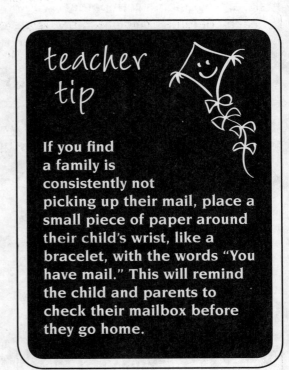

teacher tip

If you find a family is consistently not picking up their mail, place a small piece of paper around their child's wrist, like a bracelet, with the words "You have mail." This will remind the child and parents to check their mailbox before they go home.

Parent-Teacher Conferences

Making Arrangements

Parent-teacher conferences should be held twice a year. The conference should be in person and one-on-one, and held after the parents have had some time to review any assessments of their child. Schedule the conference in advance and send home a reminder note to the parents about a week before the meeting.

Making Arrangements

Parent-teacher conferences need to be scheduled in advance so you and the parents can be prepared. The conference needs to be held in a private area free from interruptions. Parent-teacher conferences can be scheduled two different ways: first, send out letters to all the parents asking what times they are available to meet with you; or second, have a sign-up sheet posted on your parent board for the parents to write down the day and time they are available. Try to be as flexible as possible and meet with each child's parents. You may need to call and make arrangements with parents who haven't signed up for a conference. Allow enough time for each conference for parents who are chatty or have many concerns. You don't want to cut parents off, and you don't want to keep them waiting.

How to Begin and How to End

Start the conference by asking the parents if they have any questions or concerns regarding their child. By giving any assessments to the parents a few days before the conference is scheduled, the parents have the opportunity to read the assessment and write down in advance any questions they may have for you. This will open the doors of communication and encourage the parents to ask questions and talk. You should not be talking the entire time. Listen to the parents and get a feeling of what they expect from you and from their child. When you discuss the child, give a well-rounded picture instead of focusing only on the areas in which the child needs improvement or has problems. Provide concrete examples for the parents from most of the development areas. These examples will come from the portfolio and anecdotal records you have been keeping. Be honest with the parents. You do not want to give them a false picture of their child. End the conference on a positive note. Let the parent know you are always available to address questions or concerns.

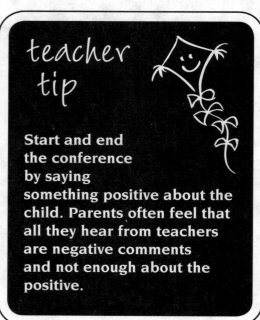

teacher tip

Start and end the conference by saying something positive about the child. Parents often feel that all they hear from teachers are negative comments and not enough about the positive.

Parent–Teacher Conferences (cont.)

Parent-Teacher Conference Sign-Up Form			
Day	Time	Parent's Name	Child's Name

Parent—Teacher Conferences (cont.)

Just a Reminder

You have signed up for a parent-teacher conference on _____

at _____ . If you are unable to attend and need

to reschedule call me at _____ .

Thank you,

_____

Volunteers

Volunteers in your class can be parents, grandparents, older siblings, or work-study high school students. If someone wants to volunteer in your class and the person has been cleared though your administration, let them. Parents are your best support and ally. Once they see how hard you work, they will have a newly found appreciation for you and your job. Have an open-door policy in which parents are welcome to help at any time of the day.

Assigning the Volunteer a Task

Ask the parents to let you know at least one day in advance if they want to come into the class and help. This way, you can have a specific task for them, such as helping with an art project, reading the book at story time, or playing a specific game with the children. Don't just let the parent or volunteer sit and observe. If they came to help, put them to work!

Before They Start

You will want to give your volunteer some tips to help him or her be successful.

- Let the volunteer know where things are in the classroom, along with the classroom rules.
- Encourage the volunteer to get down to the child's level when speaking.
- Talk normally to the children and use proper English. Don't baby-talk or talk down to the children.
- Let the children do their own work.
- Have fun.

Volunteer for Field Trips

You will need to ask for volunteers to help on field trips or for activities in the classroom. List these dates in your monthly newsletter, and either have a sign-up sheet posted or remind parents the next time that the child is dropped off or picked up at school.

Saying Thank You

Keep track of the time and day someone has helped in the classroom so you can send a thank-you note. Having parent volunteers spend time in your classroom will encourage the parents to talk to their children about activities and help them stay involved with their children's development. Be appreciative and encouraging so the volunteer will come again.

Classroom Records

Record keeping can include many things, from your anecdotal notes to how many days a child is absent and why. You will not always remember every little detail. Keeping a folder or record on each child is always a good idea.

How to Organize

Each child should have a section to hold that child's information in your file box or three-ring binder notebook. In each child's section or folder, include two pieces of paper with the child's name written on top. One paper will be labeled Health Notes such as days absent and why. The second piece of lined paper will be for behavior notes.

Behavior Notes

Include any serious conflicts between children in the behavior notes.

- For example: On Monday, June 27, Matt bit John on the back. The conflict was over the yellow dump truck. John wanted to take the truck to the sand table and Matt wanted it to stay in Block Area.
- Keeping records such as this one will allow you to go back and give a specific date and what happened. Place the note into Matt's folder.
- When you meet with Matt's parent, you can give them the dates and number of times Matt has bitten other children.

Health Notes

You may be asked, "Remember when Johnny was out with pinkeye? Do you have the dates he was out? Miranda now has it and the mother thinks she got it here at school?" You can then look into Johnny's folder on the health paper and say, "He had it six weeks ago and was out for four days." Then Miranda's parents will know she didn't get pinkeye at school.

teacher tip

Keep all private family information in a spot where it is not accessible to other parents.

Classroom Records (cont.)

Behavior Notes

Child's Name: _____

Date/Behavior: _____

_____

_____

Date/Behavior: _____

_____

_____

Date/Behavior: _____

_____

_____

Date/Behavior: _____

_____

_____

Date/Behavior: _____

_____

_____

Date/Behavior: _____

_____

_____

Date/Behavior: _____

_____

_____

Classroom Records (cont.)

Health Notes

Child's Name: _____

Date/Health: _____

_____

_____

Date/Health: _____

_____

_____

Date/Health: _____

_____

_____

Date/Health: _____

_____

_____

Date/Health: _____

_____

_____

Date/Health: _____

_____

_____

Date/Health: _____

_____

_____

Behavior Management

When you hear the words "behavior management," you may think this refers to ways you can stop bad behavior. In reality, it is much more. Behavior management is the way you handle situations and prevent conflicts that occur in your class. Start by having a clean and well-organized classroom. Children respond to well-defined areas and organization.

Encouraging Conflict Resolution

If a conflict between two children does occur, encourage the children to work it out. The children may not know what they want to say. For the first few months, you will need to model the proper problem-solving techniques.

- Have the children come face-to-face and tell one another why they are upset.
- Encourage the children to listen to one another without interrupting.
- Then ask the children, "How are you going to solve this?"
- If they come up with a solution, you need to honor it, even if it seems unfair.

The important point here is that they worked together and came up with a solution that they are both comfortable with. Bringing the children face-to-face also requires them to look at one another and see how the other is feeling. This is one step in growing out of the egocentric stage.

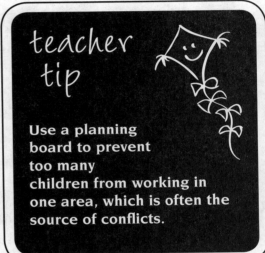

teacher tip

Use a planning board to prevent too many children from working in one area, which is often the source of conflicts.

Sharing versus Waiting Your Turn

Often you will here, "He is not sharing!" Depending on what it is, a child should not be expected to give something away to someone just because the other child wants it.

- For example: Jenny is using the pink blanket to cover her baby doll and Shelby wants it. So Shelby comes to you and says Jenny is not sharing. Do you make Jenny give the blanket to Shelby? No, you tell Shelby to ask Jenny if she can have the pink blanket when she is done. Shelby then returns to Jenny and says, "Jenny, can I have the pink blanket when you are done?"

Often the child will give the item to the other child right away. Taking turns is just as important as learning to share.

- Another example: Billy is at the art table drawing a rainbow. He has all the markers in his left hand as he draws with his right. Matt comes over and needs the blue marker that Billy is holding and Billy says, "No, I am going to use it for my rainbow." Do you tell Billy to share the markers? Yes, Billy only needs one marker at a time.

Behavior Management (cont.)

Group-Time Behaviors

Circle Time is another time in the day where you might encounter unacceptable behavior. By using sit-upons (a floor mat, cushion, carpet samples, etc.) you have the freedom to move children around. Separating children who are being distracting to one another or placing a child right next to you are quick and often successful strategies in eliminating the undesirable behavior. If the children are struggling through Circle Time and you feel that all you are doing is trying to stop behaviors, stop Circle Time. Either the children do not understand what the circle topic is about or you have gone too long.

Being Responsible for Actions and Behavior

Encourage the children to take responsibility for their actions.

- If a child is throwing a fit to get what he or she wants, allow the child to do so.
- Tell the child, "I can see you are upset. You can sit here until you are done and then we can talk about it." You have then given the child the power to determine how long he or she sits there.
- Encourage the rest of the class to ignore the behavior.
- If other behaviors occur during the fit, such as throwing things, tell the child it is okay to be mad, but it is unacceptable to throw things. Again give the power back to the child and let the fit continue as long as he or she likes.
- If the fit is going on for more than a minute, return to the child and ask if he or she is ready to talk. If so, proceed with conversation and problem solving. If the child says no, return to the rest of the group.
- If you have a child who is constantly throwing fits by using this method, do not give in to crying. The child will realize that he or she is wasting time, and fits will slowly diminish.

Tips for Behavior Management

- **Pick your battles wisely.** Do not get into power struggles with the children. It will only make matters worse. If you do become involved in a confrontation, stay calm, use the same tone of voice, and repeat the behavior you would like to see. For example, "Johnny, line up." "Johnny, line up." "Johnny, line up." Repeat it until the child stops arguing and does what is expected.
- **Be firm, fair, and consistent.** Use your firm voice only when needed. Be fair to all the children and don't change the consequences without letting the children know.
- **Don't give your power away.** You are the ultimate authority in your class. Sending the children to the office or threatening to call the parents only gives your power away. The child will begin to see the director or parent as the authority and not you. Reserve your back-up consequences for extreme cases.
- **Praise with positive words and gestures.** State the behavior you want to see and praise the children who do what is asked or expected. A gesture such as patting the child on the back or giving the child a wink is positive reinforcement.

Classroom Rules

An early childhood classroom is a place for adventure, discovery, and learning. Limits and rules are what make all of this possible. Children feel most comfortable and able to learn when they know what is expected of them and have reasonable boundaries. Teaching young children how to function in the class with an established set of rules is essential in creating harmony. When enforcing your classroom rules, remember to be firm, fair, and consistent. If you do not let Johnny and Matt have a pillow fight, then Emily and Jennifer can't have one either and the consequence must be the same for both sets of children.

When establishing a written list of rules, limit them to no more than seven. This way, the children don't feel overwhelmed. Keep your rules positive. Avoid using *no*. State the behavior you want to see, not the ones you don't.

Our Class Rules (stated positively)	Our Class Rules (stated negatively)
• Inside talking voices • Walking feet • Helping hands • Friendly faces and words • Raise a quiet hand at circle • Use materials appropriately	• No yelling • No running • No pushing or hitting • No name calling • No talking at circle without being called on • No breaking toys

Praise Does Wonders

Praise the children who are working together, listening, standing in line the correct way, sitting at circle, cleaning up, and being a good friend. Praise will go a long way. For example, the children are lined up to go outside. There are a few children tickling one another and talking. By simply saying, "I like the way I can see Alyssa's eyes." You will instantly see other children turning to look at you. At circle you can say, "Wow, look at the way Billy is sitting today." Be as positive as you can.

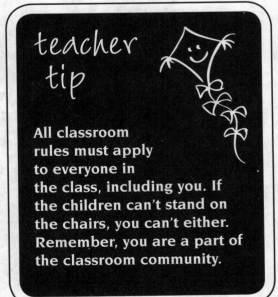

teacher tip

All classroom rules must apply to everyone in the class, including you. If the children can't stand on the chairs, you can't either. Remember, you are a part of the classroom community.

Classroom Rules

- **Inside Talking Voices**
- **Walking feet**
- **Helping hands**
- **Friendly faces and words**
- **Raise a quiet hand at circle**
- **Use materials appropriately**

#50052—*Managing an Effective Early Childhood Classroom* © *Shell Education*

Setting Reading Foundations

If you ask parents when children begin to read, many will say in the first grade. Their answers, most likely, will be based on when they remember receiving formal reading instruction. We know, though, that the foundations for learning to read are laid far before students are presented with formal reading instruction in elementary school.

Additionally, the standards movement has set high standards at each grade level, and often, what was previously taught at a higher grade level has been moved down to a lower grade level. More and more, children are expected to come to kindergarten with skills that were previously taught in kindergarten, thus putting more academic demands on early-childhood classrooms.

In 2000, the National Reading Panel published a report titled, "Teaching Children to Read: An Evidenced-Based Assessment of Scientific Research Literature on Reading and Its Implications for Reading Instruction—Reports of Subgroups." The report identified what research has shown to be the key elements of reading instruction—Phonemic Awareness, Phonics, Vocabulary, Comprehension, and Fluency.

Ensuring students have skills necessary to succeed in elementary school has become an important part of managing early-childhood curriculum. By being aware of the essential elements of reading instruction and through purposeful planning, early childhood educators can have great success in setting reading foundations as they teach reading-related skills. Key components that help children feel confident in their venture into reading are to have a print-rich environment, to model reading, and to provide plenty of opportunities to practice reading and reading-related skills in a safe, non-threatening environment. Additionally, teachers can provide purposeful encounters with reading in a variety of situations. This chapter provides ideas and activities for helping young children begin to understand how our written language is organized and used in reading situations.

teacher tip

Include developmentally-appropriate reading activities on the monthly newsletter you send home. Parents appreciate being able to make connections to activities in school and want to know how to help their children.

Setting Reading Foundations (cont.)

Environmental Print

Using environmental print is an excellent springboard for teaching reading skills. Environmental print is print that children encounter in the world around them, such as on cereal boxes, food product labels, street signs, store names, and toy packaging. Children often recognize the words in environmental print. In fact, environmental print is often one of the first things that children believe they can "read." However, the environmental print is often only recognizable to the children within its context. For example, a student may recognize the name of a restaurant on the sign outside the restaurant; however, he or she may not be able to recognize the name if it is typed on a piece of paper. Part of the recognition of the word comes in the type style and color that is typically used in the restaurant's logo.

Through interaction with an adult, such as a teacher or parents, children can use this meaningful print to make language connections that transfer to their understandings of reading other printed works. Environmental print is easy for the children to bring to the classroom, which provides an excellent opportunity for reading-related lessons using the environmental print. Additionally, environmental print can be a highly effective tool for reading-related instruction because it is particularly meaningful to students.

A key to using environmental print in the classroom is selecting environmental print the children will recognize. Popular name brands, restaurant names, and store names work well for teaching with environmental print. Encourage the children to bring environmental print they can read. This encourages the children to pay attention to the print they encounter at home and in the community. It also makes any lessons using the environmental print more meaningful.

Because teaching with environmental print can be especially effective in an early childhood classroom, each of the key reading components described in this section also provides an environmental-print connection.

teacher tip

Have a designated place for the children to put environmental print they bring from home. A bulletin board specifically for environmental print works well because the other children can see and read the words while you are waiting to use them in a lesson.

Phonemic Awareness

Phonemic awareness refers to a child's ability to identify and manipulate sounds in language. Phonemic awareness is important because research has shown that it is an excellent predictor of reading success.

A *phoneme* is a single or individual sound in language. For example, the first sound /h/ in the word *hat* is a phoneme. A phoneme does not necessarily have to be only one letter though. The /th/ sound in the word *thin* is a phoneme as well.

There are eight different categories of phonemic awareness activities:

- **Phoneme Isolation**—recognizing the sounds in words

For example: The first sound in *cat* is /c/.

- **Phoneme Identity**—recognizing words that have similar sounds

For example: The words *dog*, *dot*, and *dig* begin with /d/.

- **Phoneme Categorization**—recognizing words that sound the same and words that sound different

For example: The words *sit*, *bit*, and *hit* have similar sounds. The word *man* sounds different.

- **Phoneme Blending**—combining spoken phonemes into words

For example: The sounds /t/ /e/ /n/ make the word *ten*.

- **Phoneme Segmentation**—breaking words into their separate phonemes

For example: There are four sounds in the word *bank*—/b/ /a/ /n/ /k/.

- **Phoneme Deletion**—identifying a new word when a phoneme is removed from another word

For example: If you take away /n/ from *nice*, you get the word *ice*.

- **Phoneme Addition**—identifying a new word when a phoneme is added to another word

For example: If you add /s/ the beginning of *at*, you get the word *sat*.

- **Phoneme Substitution**—changing a phoneme in a word to make a new word

For example: If you change /p/ in *pig* to /w/, you get the word *wig*.

The phonemic awareness activities listed above are generally thought to be in order from easiest to most difficult. Although as an early childhood educator you may never present a formal lesson on phoneme substitution, it is important to be aware of the kinds of tasks students will ultimately need to be able to perform. Also, you just may have students who are easily able to perform the basic phonemic awareness activities and need a challenge.

The best part of phonemic awareness activities is that they engage children because they are fun—they are engaged in play with language.

Phonemic Awareness (cont.)

Children love to play word games with their names. Build on this by including name-related phonemic awareness activities into your day.

Nursery Rhyme Names

Have the students identify names in the nursery rhymes read in class. For example, students should identify the name *Miss Muffet* from the nursery rhyme *Little Miss Muffet*. Then, have the students identify the beginning sound of the words *Miss* and *Muffet*. Finally, have any student whose name also begins with the same sound stand. This activity can be done with the names of characters from storybooks as well.

Mystery Name

Have the students guess about whom you are speaking by segmenting a child's name. For example, if you want to call on *Tim*, rather than calling his name, call out /t/ pause /i/ pause /m/. Have the class guess which student you are naming.

New Name Game

Use the letters of the alphabet and the corresponding sounds in a name sound substitution activity. Have the students substitute the sound for the letter your class is studying for the first sound of each of their names. For example, if you are studying the letter **S**, the name *Julia* would become the name *Sulia* and *Mark* would become *Sark*. Practice with a few names each day during Circle Time or have a day on which all the students go by their new names.

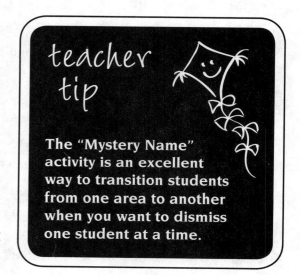

teacher tip

The "Mystery Name" activity is an excellent way to transition students from one area to another when you want to dismiss one student at a time.

Environmental Print Connection

Display a logo (without the word) of a restaurant or store with which the students will be very familiar. Ask the students if they know the name of the restaurant (or store) the logo represents. Once the restaurant (or store) has been identified, ask students to say the first sound they hear in the name of the restaurant (or store). If the students have a difficult time isolating the initial sound in the word, model saying the word very slowly or segmenting each sound in the word. Emphasize the sound made at the beginning of the word. If the student(s) still cannot identify the sound, tell him or her the sound and then say the word again several times.

Phonics

Instruction in phonics helps students make the connection between letters and sounds, as well as how letters and sounds work together to form words when reading. Young children are learning the letters of the alphabet. Many preschools have taken on the task of formally teaching students the letter names and associated sound(s). In fact, some preschools are adopting formal reading programs from textbook publishers. Although phonics instruction is traditionally thought of as a paper-pencil task, there are many developmentally-appropriate ways for students to practice identifying letters and sounds in the early childhood classroom without ever lifting a pencil.

Newspaper Hunt

Write the letter about which you are learning on a large piece of construction paper or butcher paper, for example, the letter **B**. Provide the students with newspapers and advertisements, scissors, and glue. Have the students search through the newspapers and advertisements in search of examples of the upper- and lowercase letter. If desired and appropriate, have the students find pictures that begin with the same letter. The children should then cut out the letters or pictures and glue them on the piece of paper. Display the letter/picture chart in the classroom. Of course, if students are not yet comfortable with scissors, allow them to tear out the letters, or solicit adult assistance with this activity. As an alternative, you might have the students trace the letters they find with a finger or a crayon.

Letter Tower

Rinse out and dry empty soda cans. Cover the soda cans with construction paper or contact paper. Write a different letter on the outside of each can with a thick black marker. Stack the cans in a tower. The configuration of the tower does not matter; the students just need a target. Have a student stand several feet away and throw a beanbag or light ball at the tower. The student then identifies the letter written on each can as he or she picks it up and rebuilds the tower. Extend the activity, if the student is able, by having him or her identify the sound or a word that begins with the sound.

Environmental-Print Connection

Set out a supply of environmental print. Be sure several of the environmental print words begin with the same letter. Select one of the words and display it. Ask the children to identify the name of the initial letter in the word. Tell the students the sound the letter makes as well. Sort the words based on the initial letter. Glue the sorted words onto a sheet of construction paper or butcher paper and display them in the classroom.

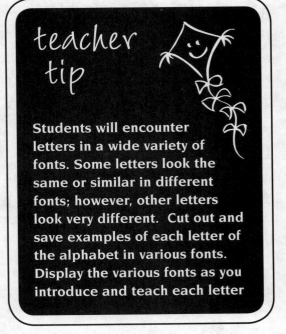

teacher tip

Students will encounter letters in a wide variety of fonts. Some letters look the same or similar in different fonts; however, other letters look very different. Cut out and save examples of each letter of the alphabet in various fonts. Display the various fonts as you introduce and teach each letter

Phonics (cont.)

Provide multi-sensory activities in which students can participate to help them become more familiar with the letters of the alphabet. Adapt the activities based on the students' familiarity with the letters of the alphabet. Narrow the task for students who are not as familiar with the letters of the alphabet by asking them to focus on one or two letters. Challenge students who are familiar with the letters of the alphabet by asking them to sound out simple consonant-vowel-consonant words.

Shaving Cream

Place a cookie tray and a can of shaving cream at a table or in a center. Demonstrate for the children how to shake the shaving cream and to spray a small amount onto the cookie tray. Allow students to visit the center and practice writing letters of the alphabet in the shaving cream.

Pipe Cleaners

Provide a small bucket of pipe cleaners for the children to use to practice forming letters. The children can either form a letter with one pipe cleaner or they can twist several pipe cleaners together to from a letter.

Hair Gel Bags

Squeeze hair gel into gallon-sized re-sealable plastic bags. Place some food coloring in the bags as well, if desired. Seal the bags tightly and place them on a flat surface, such as a table or cookie sheet on the floor. Allow the children use their fingers to practice writing letters on the plastic bags.

Magnetic Alphabet

Provide magnetic letters and a cookie sheet or other magnetic surface with which the students can experiment. Students can use the letters to spell each other's names, place the letters in alphabetical order, or if they are able, form words they know.

Letter Objects

Write the letter of the alphabet that your class is currently studying on a piece of construction paper, one per student. Provide objects corresponding to the featured alphabet letter for the students to glue around the shape of the letter. For example, when learning about the letter **J**, students can form the letter **J** with jellybeans.

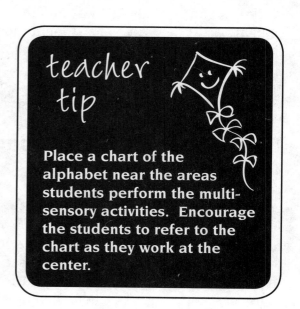

teacher tip

Place a chart of the alphabet near the areas students perform the multi-sensory activities. Encourage the students to refer to the chart as they work at the center.

Fluency

Fluency refers to a readers' ability to recognize and read words quickly and accurately. Fluency also has to do with the expression a reader uses as well. Obviously, most children in an early childhood classroom will not be able to read enough to apply this definition of fluency; however, there are many activities that can be done to set the groundwork for fluency for when students do begin reading. Modeling fluent reading is one of the most important things a teacher can do. Ask students to pay attention to the way in which you read stories, poems, and nonfiction works. Discuss with the students the way your voice sounded after reading a selection.

Variety is the Spice of Life

Children need to hear a wide variety of texts read to them. Storybooks are extremely important to children of this age; however, be sure to expose your students to chapter books, nonfiction, poetry, age-appropriate magazine or newspaper articles, cartoon strips, and more. Reading a variety of genres offers experience in hearing different vocabulary, phrasing, and even expressions.

Nursery Rhymes

Read and reread nursery rhymes to the class. These short poems are easy for children to memorize. Although it is from memory when children recite nursery rhymes, this is how students begin to develop an understanding of the natural rhythm and flow of language.

Patterned Texts

Select books with patterned text. Children quickly pick up on the language patterns and begin reciting the repeating parts of the text along with you as you read. The children are listening to the reader read with good fluency. In addition, as the children participate while chiming in with the repeating parts of the book, they are practicing good phrasing and expression as well. You will often hear children "reading" these books on their own in the classroom library with similar expression as you used in the initial reading.

teacher tip

Providing books on tape or CD to which the children can listen is an excellent opportunity for them to hear fluent reading.

Environmental-Print Connection

Gather a supply of environmental print words with which the children will be familiar. Place the words in a bag. Ask one student to select a word from the bag and tell the class a sentence using the word. Then, repeat the sentence several times using different phrasing and expression each time. Ask the students to repeat the version that sounds the most natural.

Vocabulary

The words we know and use in communication make up our vocabularies. Developing vocabulary is an important component of setting reading foundations because we know that vocabulary is directly linked to reading comprehension. The more developed a child's vocabulary is, the more likely he or she is to draw on that rich vocabulary when reading, writing, and speaking.

Model Vocabulary

One of the most important things you can do to help develop your students' vocabularies is to model a rich vocabulary. Teaching young children does not mean that you have to water down the words you use. In fact, be consciously aware of the words you select in order to model appropriate ways and contexts to use words. If you feel the children need more explanation of a particular word, include the definition within the context of what you say, rather than selecting an easier word. For example, if you want to use the word *galoshes*, you could say, "He put on his *galoshes* which are his *rain boots*."

Realia

Children learn a great deal about new words, especially nouns, when they have an opportunity to "experience" the word. Try consciously to introduce one new word a day. Think about objects with which students may not be familiar as you make your lesson plans each week. In fact, you may want to list the vocabulary word you wish to introduce each day in your lesson plans.

Often, simply by bringing an object from home or by digging it out of the back of the closet at school, students gain a whole new perspective on your lesson. The word you are using, and often even abstract concepts, become more familiar and easier to understand. For example, if a story you read tells about what a boy sees when he looks through binoculars, bring a pair of binoculars for the children to see and possibly use. Consider selecting items to bring in that are based on books you plan to read, units of study, or even just common or unusual objects, such as a compass or a lime. As you display the object, engage the students in a discussion about it. Soliciting students' experiences with the object is a great way for students to model vocabulary for each other.

teacher tip

Reading aloud daily is another excellent way to expose your class to vocabulary. Select books that are rich with vocabulary. In this way, students hear vocabulary words used in a variety of sentences and contexts.

Vocabulary (cont.)

Language Experience

Provide language experiences for small groups of children. Bring an item for the children to "experience." The object for a language experience can be any object; however, if you can relate it to something the class is studying, the object and the related vocabulary becomes more meaningful and more immediately applicable. Some examples of excellent language experience objects are listed below.

- a coconut
- jacks
- a funnel
- earmuffs
- a pinecone
- a magnifying glass
- a whisk
- a horseshoe
- shells

Encourage the children to describe the object with their five senses. Document the language the students use while they talk about the object by writing it on a board or on a piece of chart paper. Encourage each child to write or dictate a sentence about the object. Then, allow each child time to illustrate a picture to match the sentence.

Categories

Understanding how words are associated can be a challenging task for young children. Provide lots of practice in making associations by playing categorizing games. Display several items for the children. Ask the children to observe the items and try to select two or three that belong together because they share a common characteristic.

Another way to play categorizing games is to provide the name of the category and ask the children to provide the names of things that would fit in the category. One way to fit this activity into a busy schedule is to call out a category, such as "things that are cold," prior to having the children line up for lunch. As you call on each child to line up at the door, he or she must name something that is in the category. Require that each child name a different object than was previously named, if desired.

Categories

- Things for a baby
- Jewelry
- Sports
- Things you turn on
- Things you can read
- Animals that live on land
- Parts of the body
- Things that tickle
- Vehicles

Environmental-Print Connection

Display a collection of environmental print words. Ask the children if they can identify or "read" each of the words. Ask the students if they can think of ways in which the words can be grouped together. For example, the students may group together all the environmental print words that belong to food items. In this way, students are practicing the categorization of words.

Comprehension

Gaining meaning from what we read is the whole reason we read. Although most students in an early childhood class will not be reading, teachers can do a great deal to help students develop comprehension of materials that are read to them.

Thinking Aloud

Thinking aloud is a strategy in which the teacher models what he or she is thinking while reading by saying it out loud for the children to hear. For example, when showing the cover of a book, the teacher may say, "When I look at this cover I see a boy in a bathing suit. It makes me think that he will go swimming in this story." By saying out loud what you are thinking, the children begin to see the things you do in order to make meaning from the story. By doing this each time you read a story to the children, they will see a variety of comprehension strategies modeled throughout the year. You need not use this strategy on every page; however, a couple of times per book will work well.

Making Connections

Making connections to prior knowledge is an excellent way for children to make meaning from a text. There are two specific ways children can make connections—from text-to-life and from text-to-text. When children make these connections, they are bringing their prior knowledge to the text, including vocabulary, in order to better comprehend the text currently being read. Model each of these types of connections over the period of several weeks and then encourage the students to make the connections, too.

<table>
<tr><td>

Text-to-Life Connections

When children make text-to-life connections, they see similarities between what they are reading and something they have experienced. For example, you may say, "When the boy went to the beach, it reminded me of the time I went to the beach. I built a sandcastle in the sand and then the water came up and ruined it."

</td><td>

Text-to-Text Connections

In a text-to-text connection, the children make a connection between what they are currently reading and something else they have read. For example, to model a text-to-text connection, you may say, "When we read the story, Make Way for Ducklings, it reminded me of the story, A House for Hermit Crab. In both stories, animals were looking for a good home."

</td></tr>
</table>

Environmental-Print Connection

Children at this age are beginning to develop an understanding of story structure, which aids comprehension. Telling their own stories can help children understand that stories have a beginning, middle, and ending. Place a collection of environmental print words that students will easily recognize in a bag. Have a student select one of the words and tell a brief story with a beginning, middle, and ending, using the word.

Gathering Data

Before assessing a child, first determine the purpose of the assessment, or why the child is being assessed. The purpose can be for placement, progress, or curriculum planning. When completing an assessment, the physical, cognitive, and social growth of each individual child must be considered. If you are assessing the children for placement, this could be as simple as deciding which small group to put the children in. Curriculum assessment is used to determine the goals of your class or program and also the children's strengths and weakness.

The best way of assessing a young child's progress is through observation and keeping samples of the child's work. In early childhood classrooms, standardized tests and report cards are not appropriate. Progress assessment should look at the individual child and not compare the child to his or her peers. Each child, especially young children, will go through the learning process at his or her own pace.

When to Assess Skills

Assessing skills or observations are usually done twice a year.

- The first assessment should be done at the beginning of the school year. This assessment will show the child's skill level when he or she enters your classroom. It will also help in determining the goals for the individual child and where you need to begin with the class.
- The second observation is done at the end of the school year or just before the child is to move on to the next class. By comparing the two observations, the parents will see growth in all areas of development.

Portfolios

- Portfolios give the parents concrete samples of their child's work, providing focus on the child's accomplishments. The parents will be able to see firsthand the improvements and the progress their child is making.
- Dates should always be included, along with a wide variety of samples.
- The portfolio may include crayon pictures, chalk drawings, paper cuttings, sculptures, writing samples, and photographs of the child working.
- Do not include every piece of art the child has done in class; keep only the pieces that the child is extremely proud of, and works that show concentration, creativity, and improvement.
- Keep the portfolios in a file box sorted by the children's names. Keep the portfolio box separate from your daily art box.

Gathering Data (cont.)

Anecdotal Records

Along with concrete samples of the child's work, anecdotal records may also be placed in a child's portfolio.

- An anecdotal note or record is when you document what the child has done in a measurable form, without providing your opinion. For example: "May 23, 2006—Matt built a tower today by using square and rectangular blocks. When he was finished constructing, he counted how many blocks tall it was. He was able to count up to 15 without any help." The anecdotal record shows Matt constructed a tower using only two shapes and was able to count to 15.
- Document only measurable, positive, and data-proving progress.

Observations

Observations are when you observe and document what the children in your class can do.

This should be done twice a year.

- Observations are different from anecdotal records in the way in which you are presenting the information to the parents and in the way you are obtaining the information.
- Observations take time, and require you to focus on one child for an extended period of time, observing and documenting the child's abilities in all areas of development.
- Playing games and requiring a child to sit in front of you while he or she performs a task is necessary in order for you to get an accurate assessment.
- Always include the date of the assessment and the age of the child performing the tasks.
- You will document the child's growth and abilities, including gross motor, small motor, cognitive, and social-emotional.

Gross Motor	Fine Motor
• Gross motor refers to a child's ability to move the entire body and spatial awareness. • Gross-motor or large-motor skills include the ability to hop, jump, skip, run, and climb.	• Fine motor refers to a child's ability to use and have control over the small muscles in his or her hands. • This is essential in being able to color, write, paint, and cut.
Cognitive	**Social-Emotional**
• Show concentration in an activity. • Complete a task. • Know the classroom procedure. • Recognize shapes, colors, and eventually letters of the alphabet.	• Interacts with peers. • Separates from parents. • Respects the teacher. • Takes turns. • Uses materials appropriately.

Types of Assessments

There are several different forms of observational assessments. They can come in the following forms: checklist, rating scale, frequency scale (example: *sometimes, often, never*), and outline forms.

Checklist

- The checklist assessment requires you to check the box if the child can do the task.
- This type of assessment doesn't leave room for comments.
- It tends not to show a range of development.
- It is either "Yes, the child can do this skill" or "No, the child is unable to do this skill."

Rating Scale

The rating scale form requires you to circle a number—for example, 1–5—that represents how well a child can perform a task:

- 1: the child does not perform the task.
- 5: the child has mastered the skill.
- This type of form gives you a range and allows you to show the parents that the child has come close to mastering the skill or needs more practice.

Frequency Scale (Always, Sometimes, Never)

The next type of assessment is one on which you can mark *always, sometimes,* or *never* in regard to the child's frequency in performing a task.

- This gives you more flexibility than the checklist form.
- The categories of *always, sometimes,* and *never* give a bit more information to the parents. For example: Johnny is being observed catching a ball. He catches the ball four out of the 10 times.
- On the checklist form, you would have to mark "No" because Johnny hasn't mastered the skill. However, on the frequency scale, you can mark *sometimes.* Johnny needs practice at catching, but in your observation of him, he was able to catch the ball some of the time.

The following assessments are examples. The first one is done at the beginning of the year and the second is to be done just before a child goes to kindergarten.

Developmental Skills Checklist Assessment

Prekindergarten—Fall

Name: _____ Age: _____

Date: _____ Teacher: _____

Begin Here: making check boxes to the right of the skill

Social Development:		Art:	
Uses equipment appropriately		Enjoys participation	
Respects the teacher		Tries different media	
Interacts well with peers		**Small motor Skills:**	
Shows empathy for others		Uses scissors appropriately	
Takes turns		Holds pencil properly	
Listens to others		Uses crayons and markers	
Shares within developmental norms		Uses manipulatives	
Helps with classroom jobs		Attempts to tie shoes	
Is able to make choices		Buttons, zips, and snaps	
Has special friends		**Reading and Math Readiness:**	
Emotional Development:		Recognizes own name	
Approaches new experiences with confidence		Prints own name	
Appropriately handles frustration		Recognizes letters of the alphabet	
Appropriately handles anger		Enjoys stories/listening to stories	
Verbally expresses feelings		Has concept of story sequence	
Accepts responsibility for:		Likes to create stories	
• Personal belongings		Looks at books	
• Personal behavior/safety		Participates in finger plays	
Cognitive Skills:		Counts to _____	
Knows classroom procedures		Recognizes numbers	
Calls the teacher by name		Recognizes:	
Calls other children by name		• Shapes	
Shows enthusiasm about learning		• Sizes	
Completes a task		Social Skills:	
Shows concentration on a self-chosen activity		Follows two- or three-step directions	
Maintains concentration in a group activity		**Language:**	
Comments:		Speaks clearly	
		Expresses ideas in sentences	
		Carries on a conversation with others	
		Asks questions	
		Responds to questions	
		Contributes to group discussions	

Developmental Skills Checklist
Assessment (cont.)

Prekindergarten—Fall (cont.)

Music:		Gross-Motor Skills	
Listens		Runs	
Sings		Gallops	
Enjoys instruments		Skips	
Enjoys rhythm and movement		Climbs	
Participates in group activities		Crawls	
Free Play:		Monkey-walks	
Plays educational games		Pumps legs on a swing	
Works puzzles		Rides a tricycle	
Uses building blocks		Hops on two feet	
Plays in the family life center		**Balance:**	
Enjoys dramatic play		Walks forward on a balance beam	
Enjoys sensory media		Walks backward on a balance beam	
Enjoys using modeling dough		Has hand/eye and hand/foot coordination	
		Throws a ball	
		Catches a ball	
		Kicks a stationary ball	
		Kicks a rolling ball	
		Bounces a ball	
		Keeps a balloon in the air	

Comments:

Developmental Skills Checklist Assessment (cont.)

Prekindergarten—Spring

Name: _____ Age: _____

Date: _____ Teacher: _____

Begin Here: making check boxes to the right of the skill

Fine Motor and Speech Development:		Reading and Language Arts:	
Has clear and distinct speech		Recognizes and writes own name	
Established handedness		Recognizes friends' names	
Shows control of small muscles in using crayons, painting, cutting, and writing		Recognizes basic colors	
Uses scissors appropriately		Recognizes uppercase letters	
Buttons, zips, snaps, and buckles		Recognizes lowercase letters	
Attempts to tie shoes		Writes letters of the alphabet out of order	
Uses manipulatives		Recognizes rhyming words	
Social Growth and Work Habits:		Recognizes letter sounds	
Talks freely with other children		Recognizes some sight words	
Works and plays cooperatively with others		Contributes to group stories	
Participates in organized group activities		Expresses ideas in complete sentences	
Shows respect and consideration for others		**Enrichment Activities:**	
Practices self-control		Art	
Follows classroom rules		Block building	
Performs simple classroom chores		Science	
Demonstrates self-confidence		Puzzles	
Shows concentration in group activities		Sensory media	
Contributes to group discussions		Creative dramatic play	
Follows oral directions		Plays educational games	
Works independently		Music	
Takes time with projects		Plays in family life center	
Mathematical Skills:		Molding dough	
Shows rote-counting ability			
Recognizes numerals out of sequence			
Writes numerals			
Uses positional terms (first–fifth)			
Names geometric shapes			
Makes comparisons as to size and quantity			

Developmental Skills Checklist Assessment (cont.)

Prekindergarten—Spring (cont.)

Gross Motor Skills:					
Body and spatial awareness—understanding one's body and how it works in relation to itself, other objects, and other people			Center line—the ability to perform tasks involving objects and people outside one's own space		
• Understands *over, under, through*			• Cross-walks		
• Can work within own space			• Can cross midline when batting		
Balance—the ability to assume and maintain a position of activity			Eye/hand and eye/foot—the ability to use the eyes, hands, and feet together to accomplish a given task		
• Walks forward on balance beam			• Throws a ball underhand		
• Walks backward on balance beam			• Throws a ball overhand		
Dynamic balance—the ability to maintain control of the body when suspended in the air for a length of time			• Throws a beanbag at a target		
• Jumps on trampoline			• Rides a tricycle		
• Skips			• Kicks a stationary ball		
• Jumps rope			• Kicks a rolling ball		
• Performs standing broad jump			• Bounces a ball		
Laterality—the ability to use one side, opposite sides, or upper and lower parts of the body in a smooth, rhythmic manner			Upper body strength/flexibility—the ability to be strong and flexible enough to use the body independently and as a unit to perform certain tasks		
• Pumps legs on swing			• Hangs from a bar		
• Runs			• Seal-walks		
• Gallops			• Somersaults forward		
• Monkey-walks			Tracking—the ability to perform tasks involving objects and people outside one's own space		
• Hops on two feet			• Keeps a balloon in the air		
• Hops on one foot—right			• Catches a ball from a distance of four feet		
• Hops on one foot—left					
• Crab-walks					
• Bear-walks on ladder					
Comments:					

Assessment

Developmental Skills Rating Scale Assessment

Prekindergarten—Fall

Name: _____ Age: _____

Date: _____ Teacher: _____

	1 No	2	3	4	5 Yes
Social Skills:					
Uses equipment appropriately	1	2	3	4	5
Respects the teacher	1	2	3	4	5
Interacts well with peers	1	2	3	4	5
Shows empathy for others	1	2	3	4	5
Takes turns	1	2	3	4	5
Listens to others	1	2	3	4	5
Shares within developmental norms	1	2	3	4	5
Helps with classroom jobs	1	2	3	4	5
Is able to make choices	1	2	3	4	5
Makes special friends	1	2	3	4	5
Emotional Development:					
Approaches new experiences confidently	1	2	3	4	5
Appropriately handles frustration	1	2	3	4	5
Appropriately handles anger	1	2	3	4	5
Verbally expresses feelings	1	2	3	4	5
Accepts responsibility for:					
• personal belongings	1	2	3	4	5
• personal behavior/safety	1	2	3	4	5
Cognitive Skills:					
Knows classroom procedure	1	2	3	4	5
Calls the teacher by name	1	2	3	4	5
Calls other children by name	1	2	3	4	5
Shows enthusiasm about learning	1	2	3	4	5
Completes a task	1	2	3	4	5
Shows concentration on a self-chosen activity	1	2	3	4	5
Maintains concentration in group activity	1	2	3	4	5
Art:					
Enjoys participation	1	2	3	4	5
Tries different media	1	2	3	4	5
Small motor Skills:					
Uses scissors appropriately	1	2	3	4	5
Holds pencil properly	1	2	3	4	5
Uses crayons and markers	1	2	3	4	5
Uses manipulatives	1	2	3	4	5
Attempts to tie shoes	1	2	3	4	5
Buttons, zips, and snaps	1	2	3	4	5

Comments:

Developmental Skills Rating Scale Assessment (cont.)

Prekindergarten—Fall (cont.)

Reading and Math Readiness:

Recognizes own name	1	2	3	4	5
Prints own name	1	2	3	4	5
Recognizes letters of the alphabet	1	2	3	4	5
Enjoys stories/listens	1	2	3	4	5
Has concept of story sequence	1	2	3	4	5
Likes to create stories	1	2	3	4	5
Looks at books	1	2	3	4	5
Participates in finger plays	1	2	3	4	5
Counts to _____					
Recognizes numbers	1	2	3	4	5

Recognizes:

• Colors	1	2	3	4	5
• Sizes	1	2	3	4	5
• Shapes	1	2	3	4	5
Follows two- or three-step directions	1	2	3	4	5

Language:

Speaks clearly	1	2	3	4	5
Expresses ideas in sentences	1	2	3	4	5
Carries on a conversation with others	1	2	3	4	5
Asks questions	1	2	3	4	5
Responds to questions	1	2	3	4	5
Contributes to group discussions	1	2	3	4	5

Music:

Listens	1	2	3	4	5
Sings	1	2	3	4	5
Enjoys instruments	1	2	3	4	5
Enjoys rhythms and movement	1	2	3	4	5
Participates in group activities	1	2	3	4	5

Free Play:

Plays educational games	1	2	3	4	5
Works puzzles	1	2	3	4	5
Uses building blocks	1	2	3	4	5
Plays in the family life center	1	2	3	4	5
Enjoys dramatic play	1	2	3	4	5
Enjoys sensory mediums	1	2	3	4	5
Enjoys using molding dough	1	2	3	4	5

Developmental Skills Rating Scale
Assessment (cont.)

Prekindergarten—Fall (cont.)

Gross Motor Skills:

Runs	1	2	3	4	5
Gallops	1	2	3	4	5
Skips	1	2	3	4	5
Climbs	1	2	3	4	5
Crawls	1	2	3	4	5
Monkey-walks	1	2	3	4	5
Pumps on a swing	1	2	3	4	5
Rides a tricycle	1	2	3	4	5
Hops on two feet	1	2	3	4	5

Balance:

Walks forward on a balance beam	1	2	3	4	5
Walks backward on a balance beam	1	2	3	4	5

Hand/eye and Hand/foot:

• Throws a ball	1	2	3	4	5
• Catches a ball	1	2	3	4	5
• Kicks a stationary ball	1	2	3	4	5
• Kicks a rolling ball	1	2	3	4	5
• Bounces a ball	1	2	3	4	5
• Keeps a balloon in the air	1	2	3	4	5

Comments:

Developmental Skills Rating Scale Assessment (cont.)

Prekindergarten—Spring

Name: _____ Age: _____

Date: _____ Teacher: _____

	1 No	2	3	4	5 Yes
Fine Motor and Speech Development:					
Has clear and distinct speech	1	2	3	4	5
Established handedness	1	2	3	4	5
Shows control of small muscles in using crayons, painting, cutting, and writing	1	2	3	4	5
Uses scissors appropriately	1	2	3	4	5
Buttons, zips, snaps, and buckles	1	2	3	4	5
Attempts to tie shoes	1	2	3	4	5
Uses manipulatives	1	2	3	4	5
Social Growth and Work Habits:					
Talks freely with other children	1	2	3	4	5
Works and plays cooperatively with others	1	2	3	4	5
Participates in organized group activities	1	2	3	4	5
Shows respect and consideration for others	1	2	3	4	5
Practices self-control	1	2	3	4	5
Follows classroom rules	1	2	3	4	5
Performs simple classroom chores	1	2	3	4	5
Demonstrates self-confidence	1	2	3	4	5
Shows concentration in group activities	1	2	3	4	5
Contributes to group discussions	1	2	3	4	5
Follows oral directions	1	2	3	4	5
Works independently	1	2	3	4	5
Takes time with projects	1	2	3	4	5
Mathematical Skills:					
Shows rote-counting ability	1	2	3	4	5
Recognizes numerals out of sequence	1	2	3	4	5
Writes numerals	1	2	3	4	5
Uses positional terms (first–fifth)	1	2	3	4	5
Names geometric shapes	1	2	3	4	5
Makes comparisons as to size and quantity	1	2	3	4	5

Comments:

Developmental Skills Rating Scale Assessment *(cont.)*

Prekindergarten—Spring *(cont.)*

Reading and Language Arts:

Recognizes and writes own name	1	2	3	4	5
Recognizes friends' names	1	2	3	4	5
Recognizes basic colors	1	2	3	4	5
Recognizes uppercase letters	1	2	3	4	5
Recognizes lowercase letters	1	2	3	4	5
Writes letters of the alphabet out of order	1	2	3	4	5
Recognizes rhyming words	1	2	3	4	5
Recognizes letter sounds	1	2	3	4	5
Recognizes some sight words	1	2	3	4	5
Contributes to group stories	1	2	3	4	5
Expresses ideas in complete sentences	1	2	3	4	5

Enrichment Activities:

Art	1	2	3	4	5
Block building	1	2	3	4	5
Science	1	2	3	4	5
Puzzles	1	2	3	4	5
Enjoys sensory media	1	2	3	4	5
Creative dramatic play	1	2	3	4	5
Educational games	1	2	3	4	5
Music	1	2	3	4	5
Family life center	1	2	3	4	5
Modeling Dough	1	2	3	4	5

Gross Motor Skills:

Body and Spatial Awareness—Understanding one's body and how it works in relation to itself, other objects, and other people

Understands over, under, through	1	2	3	4	5
Can work within own space	1	2	3	4	5

Balance—The ability to assume and maintain a position of activity

Walks forward on balance beam	1	2	3	4	5
Walks backward on balance beam	1	2	3	4	5
Walks over objects on the balance beam	1	2	3	4	5

Dynamic Balance—The ability to maintain control of the body when suspended in air for a length of time

Jumps on trampoline	1	2	3	4	5
Skips	1	2	3	4	5
Jumps rope	1	2	3	4	5
Performs standing broad jump	1	2	3	4	5

Laterality—The ability to use one side, opposite sides, or upper and lower parts of the body in a smooth, rhythmic manner

Pumps on swing	1	2	3	4	5

Comments:

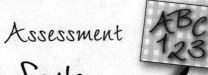

Developmental Skills Rating Scale Assessment (cont.)

Prekindergarten—Spring (cont.)

Gross Motor Skills (cont.)

Runs	1	2	3	4	5
Gallops	1	2	3	4	5
Monkey-walks	1	2	3	4	5
Hops on two feet	1	2	3	4	5
Hops on one foot—right	1	2	3	4	5
Hops on one foot—left	1	2	3	4	5
Crab-walks	1	2	3	4	5
Bear-walks on ladder	1	2	3	4	5

Tracking—The ability to perform tasks involving objects and people outside one's own space

Keeps a balloon in the air	1	2	3	4	5
Catches ball from four feet away	1	2	3	4	5

Center Line—The ability to perform tasks involving objects and people outside one's own space

Cross-walks	1	2	3	4	5
Can cross midline when batting					

Eye-hand/Eye-foot—The ability to use the eyes, hands, and feet together to accomplish a given task

Throws a ball underhand	1	2	3	4	5
Throws a ball overhand	1	2	3	4	5
Throws a beanbag at a target	1	2	3	4	5
Rides a tricycle	1	2	3	4	5
Kicks a stationary ball	1	2	3	4	5
Kicks a rolling ball	1	2	3	4	5
Bounces a ball	1	2	3	4	5

Upper Body Strength/Flexibility—The ability to be strong and flexible enough to use the body independently and as a unit to perform certain tasks

Hangs from a bar	1	2	3	4	5
Seal-walks	1	2	3	4	5
Somersaults forward	1	2	3	4	5

Comments:

Assessment

Developmental Skills Frequency Scale Assessment

Prekindergarten—Fall

Name: _____ Age: _____

Date:_____Teacher: _____

A = Always   S = Sometimes   N = Never

Social Skills:

	A	S	N
Uses equipment appropriately	☐ A	☐ S	☐ N
Respects the teacher	☐ A	☐ S	☐ N
Interacts well with peers	☐ A	☐ S	☐ N
Shows empathy for others	☐ A	☐ S	☐ N
Takes turns	☐ A	☐ S	☐ N
Listens to others	☐ A	☐ S	☐ N
Shares within developmental norms	☐ A	☐ S	☐ N
Helps with classroom jobs	☐ A	☐ S	☐ N
Is able to make choices	☐ A	☐ S	☐ N
Has special friends	☐ A	☐ S	☐ N

Emotional Development:

	A	S	N
Approaches new experiences confidently	☐ A	☐ S	☐ N
Appropriately handles frustration	☐ A	☐ S	☐ N
Appropriately handles anger	☐ A	☐ S	☐ N
Verbally expresses feelings	☐ A	☐ S	☐ N
Accepts responsibility for:			
• personal belongings	☐ A	☐ S	☐ N
• personal behavior/safety	☐ A	☐ S	☐ N

Cognitive Skills:

	A	S	N
Knows classroom procedures	☐ A	☐ S	☐ N
Calls the teacher by name	☐ A	☐ S	☐ N
Calls other children by name	☐ A	☐ S	☐ N
Shows enthusiasm about learning	☐ A	☐ S	☐ N
Completes a task	☐ A	☐ S	☐ N
Shows concentration on a self-chosen activity	☐ A	☐ S	☐ N
Maintains concentration in group activity	☐ A	☐ S	☐ N

Art:

	A	S	N
Enjoys participation	☐ A	☐ S	☐ N
Tries different media	☐ A	☐ S	☐ N

Comments:

Developmental Skills Frequency Scale Assessment (cont.)

Prekindergarten—Fall (cont.)

Small-motor Skills:

	A	S	N
Uses scissors appropriately	☐ A	☐ S	☐ N
Holds pencil properly	☐ A	☐ S	☐ N
Uses crayons and markers	☐ A	☐ S	☐ N
Uses manipulatives	☐ A	☐ S	☐ N
Attempts to tie shoes	☐ A	☐ S	☐ N
Buttons, zips, and snaps	☐ A	☐ S	☐ N

Reading and Math Readiness:

	A	S	N
Recognizes own name	☐ A	☐ S	☐ N
Prints own name	☐ A	☐ S	☐ N
Recognizes letters of the alphabet	☐ A	☐ S	☐ N
Enjoys stories/listens	☐ A	☐ S	☐ N
Has concept of story sequence	☐ A	☐ S	☐ N
Likes to create stories	☐ A	☐ S	☐ N
Looks at books	☐ A	☐ S	☐ N
Participates in finger plays	☐ A	☐ S	☐ N
Counts to _____			
Recognizes numbers	☐ A	☐ S	☐ N
Recognizes:			
• colors	☐ A	☐ S	☐ N
• sizes	☐ A	☐ S	☐ N
• shapes	☐ A	☐ S	☐ N
Follows two- or three-step directions	☐ A	☐ S	☐ N

Language:

	A	S	N
Speaks clearly	☐ A	☐ S	☐ N
Expresses ideas in sentences	☐ A	☐ S	☐ N
Carries on a conversation with others	☐ A	☐ S	☐ N
Asks questions	☐ A	☐ S	☐ N
Responds to questions	☐ A	☐ S	☐ N
Contributes to group discussions	☐ A	☐ S	☐ N

Music:

	A	S	N
Listens	☐ A	☐ S	☐ N
Sings	☐ A	☐ S	☐ N
Enjoys instruments	☐ A	☐ S	☐ N
Enjoys rhythms and movement	☐ A	☐ S	☐ N
Participates in group activities	☐ A	☐ S	☐ N

Comments:

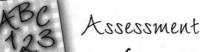
Developmental Skills Frequency Scale Assessment (cont.)

Prekindergarten—Fall (cont.)

Free Play:

	A	S	N
Plays educational games	☐ A	☐ S	☐ N
Works puzzles	☐ A	☐ S	☐ N
Uses building blocks	☐ A	☐ S	☐ N
Plays in the family-life center	☐ A	☐ S	☐ N
Enjoys dramatic play	☐ A	☐ S	☐ N
Enjoys sensory mediums	☐ A	☐ S	☐ N
Enjoys using modeling dough	☐ A	☐ S	☐ N

Gross Motor Skills:

	A	S	N
Runs	☐ A	☐ S	☐ N
Gallops	☐ A	☐ S	☐ N
Skips	☐ A	☐ S	☐ N
Climbs	☐ A	☐ S	☐ N
Crawls	☐ A	☐ S	☐ N
Monkey-walks	☐ A	☐ S	☐ N
Pumps on a swing	☐ A	☐ S	☐ N
Rides a tricycle	☐ A	☐ S	☐ N
Hops on two feet	☐ A	☐ S	☐ N

Balance:

	A	S	N
Walks forward on a balance beam	☐ A	☐ S	☐ N
Walks backward on a balance beam	☐ A	☐ S	☐ N

Hand/eye and Hand/foot coordination:

	A	S	N
• Throws a ball	☐ A	☐ S	☐ N
• Catches a ball	☐ A	☐ S	☐ N
• Kicks a stationary ball	☐ A	☐ S	☐ N
• Kicks a rolling ball	☐ A	☐ S	☐ N
• Bounces a ball	☐ A	☐ S	☐ N
• Keeps a balloon in the air	☐ A	☐ S	☐ N

Comments:

Developmental Skills Frequency Scale Assessment (cont.)

Prekindergarten—Spring

Name: _____ Age: _____

Date: _____ Teacher: _____

Speech Development:

Skill	A	S	N
Has clear and distinct speech	☐ A	☐ S	☐ N
Established handedness	☐ A	☐ S	☐ N

Social Growth and Work Habits:

Skill	A	S	N
Talks freely with other children	☐ A	☐ S	☐ N
Works and plays cooperatively with others	☐ A	☐ S	☐ N
Participates in organized group activities	☐ A	☐ S	☐ N
Shows respect and consideration for others	☐ A	☐ S	☐ N
Practices self-control	☐ A	☐ S	☐ N
Follows classroom rules	☐ A	☐ S	☐ N
Performs simple classroom chores	☐ A	☐ S	☐ N
Demonstrates self-confidence	☐ A	☐ S	☐ N
Shows concentration in group activities	☐ A	☐ S	☐ N
Contributes to group discussions	☐ A	☐ S	☐ N
Follows oral directions	☐ A	☐ S	☐ N
Works independently	☐ A	☐ S	☐ N
Takes time with projects	☐ A	☐ S	☐ N

Mathematical Skills:

Skill	A	S	N
Shows rote-counting ability	☐ A	☐ S	☐ N
Recognizes numerals out of sequence	☐ A	☐ S	☐ N
Writes numerals	☐ A	☐ S	☐ N
Uses positional terms (first-fifth)	☐ A	☐ S	☐ N
Names geometric shapes	☐ A	☐ S	☐ N
Makes comparisons as to size and quantity	☐ A	☐ S	☐ N
Recognizes and writes own name	☐ A	☐ S	☐ N
Recognizes friends' names	☐ A	☐ S	☐ N
Recognizes basic colors	☐ A	☐ S	☐ N
Recognizes uppercase letters	☐ A	☐ S	☐ N
Recognizes lowercase letters	☐ A	☐ S	☐ N
Writes letters of the alphabet (not in order)	☐ A	☐ S	☐ N
Recognizes rhyming words	☐ A	☐ S	☐ N
Recognizes letter sounds	☐ A	☐ S	☐ N
Recognizes some sight words	☐ A	☐ S	☐ N
Contributes to group stories	☐ A	☐ S	☐ N
Expresses ideas in complete sentences	☐ A	☐ S	☐ N

Comments:

Assessment

Developmental Skills Frequency Scale Assessment *(cont.)*

Prekindergarten—Spring *(cont.)*

Reading and Language Arts:
Enrichment Activities:

	A	S	N
Art	☐	☐	☐
Block building	☐	☐	☐
Science	☐	☐	☐
Works puzzles	☐	☐	☐
Enjoys sensory media	☐	☐	☐
Creative dramatic play	☐	☐	☐
Plays educational games	☐	☐	☐
Music	☐	☐	☐
Plays in family-life center	☐	☐	☐
Enjoys using modeling dough	☐	☐	☐

Fine-Motor Skills:

	A	S	N
Shows control of small muscles while using crayons, painting, cutting, and writing	☐	☐	☐
Uses scissors appropriately	☐	☐	☐
Buttons, zips, snaps, and buckles	☐	☐	☐
Attempts to tie shoes	☐	☐	☐
Uses manipulatives	☐	☐	☐

Gross-Motor Skills:

Body and Spatial Awareness—Understanding one's body and how it works in relation to itself, other objects, and other people

	A	S	N
Understands *over, under, through*	☐	☐	☐
Can work within own space	☐	☐	☐

Balance—The ability to assume and maintain a position of activity

	A	S	N
Walks forward on balance beam	☐	☐	☐
Walks backward on balance beam	☐	☐	☐
Walks over objects on the balance beam	☐	☐	☐

Dynamic Balance—The ability to maintain control of the body when suspended in air for a length of time

	A	S	N
Jumps on trampoline	☐	☐	☐
Skips	☐	☐	☐
Jumps rope	☐	☐	☐
Performs standing broad jump	☐	☐	☐

Comments:

ABC
123

Developmental Skills Frequency Scale
Assessment (cont.)

Prekindergarten—Spring (cont.)

Gross-Motor Skills (cont.):

*Laterality—The ability to use one side, opposite sides,
or upper and lower parts of the body in a smooth,
rhythmic manner*

	A	S	N
Pumps on swing	☐	☐	☐
Runs	☐	☐	☐
Gallops	☐	☐	☐
Monkey-walks	☐	☐	☐
Hops on two feet	☐	☐	☐
Hops on one foot—right	☐	☐	☐
Hops on one foot—left	☐	☐	☐
Crab-walks	☐	☐	☐
Bear-walks on ladder	☐	☐	☐

*Tracking—The ability to perform tasks involving
objects and people outside one's own space*

	A	S	N
Keeps a balloon in the air	☐	☐	☐
Catches ball from four feet away	☐	☐	☐

Appendix A

Works Cited

Chrisman, K. 2005. The nuts and bolts of discovery centers. National Science Teachers Association. ERIC Document EJ721628.

DeMarie, D. 2001. A trip to the zoo: Children's words and photographs. ERIC Document ED452997.

Friedman, S. 2005. Environments that inspire. National Association for the Education of Young Children on the Web.

Fromberg, D.P. 1998. Play Issues in early childhood education. In *The early childhood curriculum: A review of current research*, edited by C. Seefeldy. Columbus, OH: Merrill.

Gartrell, D. 2007. *A guidance approach for the encouraging classroom, Fourth Edition*. New York: Thompson Delmar Learning.

Gilbert, J.L. 2001. Getting help from Erikson, Piaget, and Vygotsky: Developing infant-toddler curriculum. ERIC Document ED457968.

Grisham-Brown, J., Hallam, R.; Brookshire, R. 2006. Using authentic assessment to evidence children's progress towards early learning standards. *Early Childhood Journal* ERIC Document EJ747265.

National Association for the Education of Young Children Position Statement 1996. Developmentally appropriate practice in early childhood programs serving children from birth-age eight. Washington DC: National Association for the Education of Young Children Publishing.

National Institute of Child Health and Human Development. 2000. Teaching children to read: An evidence-based assessment of the scientific research literature on reading and its implications for reading instruction. Report of the National Reading Panel. Washington, DC: U.S. Government Print Office.

Piaget, J. 1973. The child and reality: Problems of genetic psychology. ERIC Document 089207.

Turner, J. 2000. Parent involvement: What can we learn from research? *Montessori Life*. ERIC Document EJ621992.